Everyday Life in BibleTimes

Everyday Life in Bible Times

Third Edition

By Arthur W. Klinck

Revised by Erich H. Kiehl

CPH™

SAINT LOUIS

Edited by Arnold E. Schmidt

Write to Library for the Blind, 1333 S. Kirkwood Road, St. Louis, MO 63122-7195 to obtain these materials in braille or in large print.

The Scripture quotations in this book are from New King James Version, copyright © 1979, 1980, 1982. Used by permission.

Cover photo shows items used in everyday life in Bible times, from Abila of the Decapolis, northern Jordan. Back row: glass unguentarium (for perfumes or unguents), ceramic cook pot, unguentarium, and table vessel. Middle row: ceramic oil lamps. Front row: ceramic oil lamp and glass kohl tube (for cosmetics). Courtesy Dr. W. Harold Mare, Covenant Theological Seminary, St. Louis, Missouri, Director, Abila Excavation.

1 2 3 4 5 6 7 8 9 10   04 03 02 01 00 99 98 97 96 95

Contents

Editor's Preface

Home Life in Bible Times has served church school teachers and students of Scripture since 1947. The author, Dr. Arthur W. Klinck, died in 1959. Prior to his death he reworked the first edition to bring it up to date. His changes and additions were incorporated into the Revised (Second) Edition.

To keep *Home Life in Bible Times* current for our day, we asked Dr. Erich H. Kiehl to provide a new set of changes and additions. Dr. Kiehl has studied biblical history and archaeology extensively. Much of this study took place in Egypt, Jordan, and Palestine. He also helped Dr. Klinck's widow organize and display the dioramas on the campus of Concordia Seminary, St. Louis, Missouri.

This new edition, *Everyday Life in Bible Times,* builds the scenery that sets the stage for the study of the Old and New Testaments. The background information will enrich church school classes and personal Bible study. For example:

- Dozens of passages in Scripture use pictures related to the harvesting of grain. The material found in "Cutting and Binding the Grain" and "Threshing and Winnowing" in chapter 2 explains how harvesters carried out these procedures.
- Biblical betrothal laws and customs differ significantly from customs in most lands today. The discussion under "Betrothal and Marriage" in chapter 8 will help you better understand Abraham's arrangements for Isaac (Genesis 24:2–9), Joseph's relationship with Mary (Matthew 1:18–25), and other passages.

Everyday Life in Bible Times will help you become more familiar with life in the biblical world. May this great tool help you get into and understand the Word of God as revealed in the Scriptures.

Arnold E. Schmidt, Editor

Preface to First Edition

The text *Home Life in Bible Times: A Study in Biblical Antiquities* aims to make our church school teachers and general Bible students more familiar with the everyday life of Bible people as a background for their understanding and appreciation of the Holy Scriptures and for the improvements of their teaching of Biblical truth. ...

No apology is made for the amount of space given to the various topics treated in the text. The author's selection was largely dictated by what he considered to be the needs and interests of church school teachers as he has come to know them through his contacts with many hundreds of them in a variety of areas during the past two decades. Some important material is passed over very briefly because it has been treated so often and so fully elsewhere as to have become common knowledge. Some material has been expanded because of its special value in the personal life and teaching of the religious worker. All of it provides but a series of glimpses into the riches of God's Word in the setting of its human background. If those who read these pages privately or study them in organized classes are led just a little deeper into the beauty and instruction and comfort of the inspired writings, the author will feel richly rewarded. ...

In presenting this study the author wishes to express his deep appreciation to all those who have given him permission to study their collections or have been helpful to him in tracking down one or another small but elusive bit of information. Special gratitude is due Dr. Watson Boyes, Curator of the Oriental Institute Museum, University of Chicago; Prof. C. T. Curelly, Director of the Royal Ontario Museum of Archaeology, Toronto; Dr. H. E. Winlock, Director, and Dr. Ludlow Bull of the Metropolitan Museum of Art, New York; Mrs. Loring Dam, Curator of the Education Department, University of

Pennsylvania Museum, Philadelphia; Dr. Sidney Smith, Keeper of the Department of Egyptian and Assyrian Antiquities, British Museum, London, for permission to make a detailed study and comparison of the archaeological material under their care, along with pertinent photographs, periodicals, and books in their collections.

To his many colleagues … the author expresses his appreciation for the stimulation and encouragement which made the text seem worthwhile to begin and follow through.

A. K.

Chapter 1

Primitive Outdoor Occupations

Introduction

Man's work before and after the fall. After creating Adam, God put him into the Garden of Eden to cultivate and take care of it and thereby to live a life of wholesome activity (Genesis 2:15). Adam did everyday tasks of farming—sowing, cultivating, pruning, and gathering fruit. As he worked, Adam could find happiness and contentment. He also could make a living for himself and his family. He would know the feeling of physical well-being that comes with bodily exertion. He would experience the mental satisfaction of planning his work in advance, so that, according to God's command, he would be able to subdue the earth. (See Genesis 1:28.)

Work was necessary for humanity's well-being before the fall. It was even more necessary after sin entered the world. Now Adam and Eve began that war with nature that humanity has had to fight ever since. Sin caused the ground to suffer the curse of God. Thorns and thistles hampered human efforts. The earth no longer yielded her fruit. In the sweat of his brow Adam toiled and ate his bread. (See Genesis 3:17–19.)

Some of the blessings of work. Often Adam must have seen the need to work as a burdensome curse of God, but it was really a blessing. Through careful planning and hard labor he was able to force a living from the reluctant soil. In the fatigue that followed this hard physical exertion, he found peaceful rest. In work, too, he found an antidote for the sins of regretful brooding and despair. Work helped him curb the sinful desires of his flesh, his pride, and the urge he must often have felt to blame Eve for the fall into sin.

The sons of Adam and Eve learned to work as farmers and shepherds. Thus they divided the chief tasks of their father. Cain's work and sacrifice were in themselves no less honorable than Abel's. They failed to bring him satisfaction and blessing because his heart was not right (Genesis 4:5–7). Evidently Cain had lost his faith and trust in God. Being unrepentant and rebellious, he permitted his mind to brood over God's favorable reception of Abel's sacrifices. Abel's cheerful willingness to dedicate the firstlings of his flock to the Lord (Genesis 4:4) demonstrated his whole attitude to work and its blessings.

Ever since, as faithful and thankful people have gone about their daily tasks with intelligence and diligence, God has built them into sturdy, self-reliant characters. Such persons have escaped many of the temptations that attack those whose heart, because of ingratitude and resentment, is not in their work.

Rugged Palestine as the home of God's people. God called Abraham, the ancestor of His chosen people, to leave the rich Tigris-Euphrates Valley and live in the plains and hills of Canaan. From the Promised Land God took the patriarchal family to the fertile delta region of northern Egypt. He led their descendants in the wilderness of Sinai for a generation. These periods were seasons of preparation for their role in world history. God's people were not to be wealthy landlords or peasant slaves in Egypt or Babylonia, nor were they to become restless, wandering, fighting desert tribes. God chose for their permanent home the land of Canaan. There they could become a freedom-loving independent people, each with his own farm or his own vineyard.

The struggle for existence and its results. In Canaan God's people could make their living as shepherds. This required continuous watchfulness, industry, and faithfulness in their lonely task of caring for their flocks. Here, too, they could earn a good living from the soil, but only by long hours of hard labor. Here, too, they could grow grapes and other fruits successfully, but only by terracing the hill slopes, maintaining the stone-terraced walls, and guarding the vineyards against marauding men and animals. Only by careful planning and generations of devoted work could the country be made and kept "a good land, a land of brooks of water, of fountains and springs, that flow out of valleys and hills; a land of wheat and barley, of vines and fig trees and pomegranates, a land of olive oil and honey" (Deuteronomy 8:7–9).

In this chosen land the people of Israel were to find and work out their God-given destiny. They constantly struggled for existence. Hardy shepherds and vinedressers, farmers of the lowlands and valleys and plains, and fishermen of Galilee and of the Mediterranean coast became strong and reliant people. They were able to support themselves and to defend themselves against their enemies. Such was the task of Samuel and David, of Isaiah and Amos, of Jesus, of Peter and John, and of the apostle Paul.

The value of studying ancient customs. What was the daily life of these people? How did they earn their living? What did they eat and drink and wear? How did they find shelter from heat and cold and rain? What were their interests and social customs?

These questions are important. Bible truths apply to everyone, but the Bible itself is built around the history of a people. Its characters act according to the customs of that people. Its parables are based on their daily life and activities. As we learn about these people, we better understand Bible history. Also, we will better understand the parables, laws, sermons, and doctrines that the Holy Spirit has woven into the historical pattern of the Scriptures.

Hunting

Reasons for engaging in hunting. God told Noah and his sons that they could use animals for food (Genesis 9:3). The Bible first mentions hunting when it calls Nimrod "a mighty hunter before the Lord" (Genesis 10:9). Like Babylonian nobles, he may have hunted wild animals for sport and adventure. David, on the other hand, had to kill a lion and a

15

bear to protect his flocks (1 Samuel 17:34–37). Esau went to the field to hunt wild game from which to prepare tasty meat such as his father loved (Genesis 27:4). Other beasts of prey in Palestine included lions, panthers, hyenas, jackals, foxes, wild boars, wolves, bears, and wild dogs.

Thus, from earliest times the Hebrew people hunted wild animals and fowl to supplement their scant meat supply. By eating deer, gazelle, antelope, mountain sheep, mountain goats, and other "clean" animals, as well as the various "clean" birds, farmers could spare their domestic flocks and herds. In this way they preserved their source of milk and wool.

Weapons used in hunting. The hunting weapons mentioned in the Bible are those common to most ancient nations.

The bow and arrow appear very early in the history of God's people and throughout biblical times (Genesis 27:3).

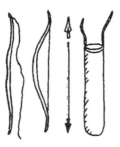   

Bows, arrowhead, arrow,   Lance, dart, quiver,
and quiver   and javelin

The *bow,* made of wood, was small compared with the powerful longbow of the later North European races. It was strung with gut, hide, sinew, or a cord made of waxed cotton or linen. The *arrows* were of about lead-pencil thickness. Made of straight reeds or cut from straight-grained wood, they were tipped with bronze or iron arrowheads. A hunter slung a *quiver,* resembling a small golf bag, over his shoulder. It could hold a dozen or more arrows.

Hunters used short spears, or *darts,* for nearby game. They used a longer spear, or *javelin,* and a *lance* for long-distance throwing. The javelin and lance, used like a modern bayonet for thrusting, were shafts of wood from three to seven feet long. They had tips of bronze or iron.

A young Israelite man could skillfully use a *sling,* which might be his six-foot sash of cloth. The slinger held one end of the sash firmly by winding it around his fingers. He gripped the other end between his thumb and forefinger. He placed a stone into the loop of the cloth. He then swung it rapidly at arm's length until, when it had attained great momentum, he released the loosely held end. The stone then flew to the target.

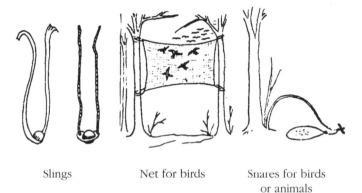

Slings   Net for birds   Snares for birds
                                       or animals

Used with an egg-size stone as a missile, the sling was a powerful weapon. It could kill dangerous wild animals. We need not be surprised that the stone slung by David sank deep into the forehead of Goliath. In his scorn for David, Goliath had failed to pull down his strong, metal helmet to protect his forehead (1 Samuel 17:49–50).

Methods used in trapping animals and birds. In order to catch the smaller animals or birds, hunters used various types of *nets* and *snares.* They might stretch a coarse-meshed net among the branches of trees along the route followed by birds in flight. They might make a noose of strong cord, one end tied to the end of a sapling that had been bent over and pegged to the ground. When a bird or animal pulled or scratched at the bait, the sapling snapped free from the peg.

As it jerked the noose upwards, it suspended the victim in midair (Jeremiah 5:26; Proverbs 7:23; Psalm 124:7; Amos 3:5).

Hunters usually caught larger animals such as gazelles, goats, lions, and jackals in *pits*. These were dug into the paths the animals usually followed as they went to drink. The pit was covered with a loose framework of small tree branches and reeds. Hunters carefully packed a thin layer of earth over them. This gave way at the slightest pressure. It threw the unsuspecting animal into the pit, where it was at the mercy of the hunter. (See 2 Samuel 23:20.)

Humane treatment of animals. To keep the supply of wild life from being exhausted, the Hebrew law declared a closed season on game animals and birds every seventh year. Animals were allowed to eat the balance of the unharvested crop after the poor had had their fill. (See Exodus 23:11 and Leviticus 25:7.)

In appreciation of God's mercy, God expected them to be merciful to animals, a lesson Christians need to impress upon their children (Psalm 104:21; 147:9; Job 38:41). The blood of animals killed for food was permitted to soak into the ground. It was not eaten but reverently covered with dust (Leviticus 17:13).

Fishing

Israelite knowledge of fishing. The Old Testament does not describe the process of fishing, but references to fishing show that the Israelites knew about it. Very likely they practiced it to supplement their meat supply (Ezekiel 47:10). In the wilderness the wandering tribes complained to Moses that he had deprived them of the fish of the river Nile (Numbers 11:5). At the time of Nehemiah, fish of the sea were sold on the market in Jerusalem (Nehemiah 13:16). One entrance to Jerusalem had already been named the "Fish Gate," no doubt because of the fish market in its vicinity (Nehemiah 12:39; 2 Chronicles 33:14).

The New Testament gives several extended accounts of fishing. Some of Jesus' disciples—Simon, Andrew, James, and

John—made their living by fishing on Lake Galilee before they began to follow Jesus. Occasionally they went back to their former occupation for a short time. (See Matthew 4:21; Luke 5:5–6; and John 21:3.)

The use of the net. About 30 varieties of freshwater fish still thrive in the Sea of Galilee. Among them are the catfish. Because they have no scales, catfish were classified as unclean and not to be eaten by God's covenant people (Leviticus 11:9–11). The largest category of native fish is the comb or "musht" fish. It is the only large fish in the lake that moves in shoals. These probably were the fish caught in the event of Luke 5:1–7. Their flat shape makes them suitable for frying. This fish became known as St. Peter's fish.

The smallest commercially important fish is the Kinneret sardine. People in Palestine and surrounding nations ate large quantities of pickled and salted fish from the Lake of Galilee. The pickling industry was located in Magdala, at the northwestern shore of the lake. Fishing was a profitable vocation.

The favorite method of fishing used nets of various types. The mesh varied from coarse to fine according to the kind of fish the people intended to catch.

A *dip net* had a cone-shaped mesh. It was held open by a wooden hoop formed from the thin end of a newly cut branch. The thicker end of the branch served as the handle.

Casting net and dip net   Dragnet between boats

Casting nets were about 10 to 15 feet in diameter. Weights around the edge pulled the net down. A fisherman pulled the center cord to narrow the net's opening until he could reach into the net to take out the fish (Isaiah 19:8; Ezekiel 32:3–4; Matthew 4:18–20). To use this net, one needed dexterity and skill.

For centuries use of the *dragnet* or seine was the most important fishing method on the lake. Made of netting, seines varied in length. Probably most were from 750 to 1,000 feet long and about 5 to 25 feet wide. The rope at the bottom was weighted with sinkers, and the rope at the top had cork floats. Ropes were attached to each end of the net to help pull it to shore. The seine was normally taken at least 300 feet from the shore—by men or by two boats—and then pulled together and drawn to the shore, usually by the men in the boat nearest the shore (John 21:3–11). Periodically the net had to be cleaned of driftwood and rubbish (Matthew 4:21–22). The dragnet is normally used in the late afternoon and into the night.

In one of His parables Jesus compares the kingdom of heaven to this type of net. Just as the dragnet brings all kinds of fish to the shore, where the fishermen separate the good from the bad, "so it will be at the end of the age. The angels will come forth, [and] separate the wicked from among the just" (Matthew 13:49).

Men on shore often "spotted" fish on the water. After the resurrection Jesus appeared to seven of His disciples after they had fished all night and had caught nothing. Serving as a "spotter," Jesus performed a miracle that allowed them to catch a tremendous number of fish (John 21:3–6). The dragnet teaches lessons in *cooperation* and *teamwork*.

Fishing with hooks. Fishhooks are mentioned in Amos 4:2; Ezekiel 29:4; Job 41:1; and Matthew 17:27. No doubt people of Israel and their neighbors used them extensively. All sizes of ancient hooks of iron and bronze have been preserved—from light ones, not over an inch long, to hooks that could catch and hold the largest fish of the Nile. Ancient fishhooks were shaped very much like those we use today. The "fishhooks" mentioned in Amos 4:2 may refer to gaffs used to pull fish from the nets into the boats.

Ancient fishhooks

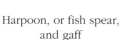

Harpoon, or fish spear, and gaff

The fish spear, or harpoon. The Egyptian fisherman permitted his boat to drift down the Nile. Statuelike, he knelt at the edge of the deck with spear poised, ready to drive it into the body of any large fish he might see. While in Egypt the Israelites certainly learned this use of spears or harpoons. However, Scripture does not mention this type of fishing in the Lake of Galilee or in the Jordan River.

Development of "apostles." Why did the small group of Jesus' disciples include so *many* fishermen, especially since Jesus Himself was "a carpenter's son"? Perhaps it was because, as fishermen, men like Peter and James and John had learned the value of hard work. They had learned to endure the disappointment of fishing a whole night and catching nothing. They had practiced patience through many a long hour of waiting. They had dared to face the treacherous storms of Lake Galilee. Jesus chose such people to become "fishers of men" (Matthew 4:19), an occupation in which they could use all the patience, strength, perseverance, and courage they had learned.

Grazing and Sheep Raising

Ranching in the east country. Much of the windswept plateau east of the Jordan River was cattle country. The "strong bulls of Bashan" (Psalm 22:12) were as proverbial as "Texas longhorns." Pasturing their cattle in the open the year round, the nomadic ranchers lived largely on meat and milk products. They supplemented their diet with wild fruits, nuts, and herbs of the field, rather than with agricultural products. They counted their wealth in cattle. The meat and hides furnished food and raw materials for export to the larger cities. Great herds of sheep, goats, and donkeys grazed on the grassy uplands and in the valleys. On the fringes of the Syrian Desert, camels were the chief source of wealth. Like Abraham, Job was a great rancher. He had vast herds of sheep, camels, oxen, and donkeys (Job 1:3).

Hog raising. Hogs, unclean according to the Mosaic law (Leviticus 11:7), were not raised by the Israelites themselves, but in the "far country" (Luke 15:13). There the lost (prodigal) son wasted his riches and finally had to try to keep alive by herding the hogs of a heathen citizen. In the country of the Gadarenes (Mark 5:11) the non-Jewish people kept pigs in large numbers.

Raising sheep and goats. In Palestine proper, west of the Jordan, the land was needed for agricultural purposes. It could not be set aside for pasture. A farmer might have a cow or two or a yoke of oxen to pull his wagon and agricultural implements. He used donkeys as beasts of burden about his farm and vineyard. In later times he might even keep one camel for the same purpose. But sheep and goats were much more numerous. They could find a living in the uncleared "wilderness" (Luke 15:4), on the steep slopes, and in the ravines of the hilly regions that were inaccessible to larger animals. Many people in the villages and towns had a few sheep or goats each. This was and is true also of inhabitants of Jerusalem. These were often herded by the village shepherd.

The equipment of the shepherd. Often the shepherd lived in a village and served as its shepherd for all or part of its sheep and goats as well as his own. He would pick them up at dawn and return them in the late afternoon (Luke 15:3–7). In certain times of the year he might care for the sheep away from the area of the village, for example, on the fringes of the wilderness of Judea, far away from the village. He then would keep the sheep in a sheepfold at night. His equipment had to be complete, yet compact and light enough to carry.

Rod and staff and horn
of oil

Shepherd's bag

To protect his sheep he needed his "rod and staff" (Psalm 23:4). The rod was a club about two feet long, sometimes with knotty knots at the thick end. The shepherd gripped the thinner end in his hand or attached the rod to his sash by a leather cord strung through a hole in the handle. This was a formidable weapon against robbers or wild animals. The shepherd used his staff to guide his sheep, to knock off twigs and leaves from the trees for their food, and to assist himself as he climbed steep and rocky hillsides and treacherous ravines in search of food, water, and shelter for his flock. The staff was a straight rod about six or seven feet long, tapered at one end. It did not have a crook, as many Western pictures show. The shepherd's crook of Christian art seems to be a European rather than a Palestinian staff.

Like the hunter, the shepherd carried his sling and a few smooth stones in his shepherd's bag for defense against marauders, animal or human. A sling had two long cords of woven goat's hair, sinews, or leather with a leather or woolen pocket fastened to them. This pocket could hold a flint or limestone about two or three inches in diameter. David used his sling to kill the giant Goliath (1 Samuel 17:40). Also, "among all this people there were seven hundred select men who were lefthanded; every one could sling a stone at a hair's breadth and not miss" (Judges 20:16).

The shepherd's bag also held his lunch of dried figs, olives, raisins, cheese and bread, or parched wheat. At his sash hung a clay flask or a hollow gourd. In it he carried water or milk. He might pack a horn of olive oil in the same way. He draped his heavy cloak of sheepskin, goat hair, or camel hair—or of homespun wool—over his shoulders. A sash at the waist held it in place. The cloak became a coat by day and a cover by night. In the fold above his sash he could find room for a sick or injured lamb (Isaiah 40:11) that would have perished without his help. On his head he wore a square cotton cloth folded into a triangle and held in place about his temples by a woven cord of wool. Thus equipped, the shepherd was ready to battle the elements or his enemies for days or even weeks at a time.

In addition to essential equipment a shepherd often carried a reed pipe. On it he played simple, haunting music.

Pottery flask and gourd
of water

Cave sheepfold

The construction of the sheepfold. The sheepfold might be a cave reaching far back into the limestone cliff. Such caves have been occupied in Palestine by successive generations of shepherds since the days of Israel's predecessors, the Canaanite tribes. In front of the cave the shepherd might build a wall of rock, about six feet high. It had only one door through which he and his sheep could enter (John 10:1). Sometimes the wall had thorns or pieces of glass or metal planted along the top to keep out marauding wolves or thieves. Thus the sheep had a warm stable and an open courtyard, where they could be protected from their enemies. Yet in pleasant weather they could sleep in the open air under the stars.

When Gad and Reuben inherited the east country before Palestine was conquered, they built sheepfolds for the protection of their flocks (Numbers 32:16). Where caves were not available, the shepherd built his enclosing wall of rock in the same way. He roofed it over at

Sheepfold built of rock

one end to make a weatherproof stable for the sheep. One reached the interior of the stable through archways opening into the court. Such a sheepfold, surrounded by its stone wall and defended by the shepherds, became a fortress for the protection of the sheep.

The Shepherd and His Sheep

Pasturing the sheep. The hills and mountains of Judea had few safe, open meadows where sheep could be left unguarded by day or night. In the daytime the shepherd searched for the best pasture, in the recesses of a winding ravine or on a grassy slope. He could reach this pasture only by carefully leading the sheep over dangerous mountain paths. He led them to the still waters, where they could drink without falling into a swift current. Often he had to pull water out of a well or cistern. He poured this into stone troughs surrounding the well. He let his sheep rest in the shade of the trees or where some great rock cast a welcome shadow (Isaiah 32:2). While they rested, he watched, either sitting on a rock or leaning on his staff, always within their sight. Should they become frightened, they might stampede. Meanwhile he might be playing simple music on a shepherd's pipe, which he could lay aside in a second to free his hands to use his sling or club.

Back to the fold. A shepherd had to be able to read the signs of the sky. At the first sign of a threatening storm, or by midafternoon, he called his sheep together and headed for home. He did not want to risk their lives in a sudden flood or in the darkness.

A shepherd did not drive his sheep. Instead, he walked ahead of them, calling gently to those that showed signs of weariness and carefully seeing that each wanderer returned to the flock. Then, standing in his sheepfold doorway, he called them by name. They entered the sheepfold by walking between his legs. As they did so, he checked them for injuries and insects. A single shepherd could care for 30 to 40 sheep. If he had more, he would need a helper or two. (See Luke 15:3–7.)

Dangers of the night. Not all danger left when the shepherd had led his sheep into the fold. The enemy might strike at night, so the shepherd watched over his flocks from the top of the wall or roof, or he dozed by his campfire while the flock slept. When weather permitted, he might sleep at the door of the sheepfold to protect his flock from intruders. When robbers or wolves attacked, a faithful shepherd did not flee, but was ready to give his life for his sheep. He bravely stood up against his enemies until either he or they were defeated.

The Good Shepherd. What a picture the shepherd passages give us of the Savior! No wonder the Lord chose this picture to explain the relationship between Himself and His people. His hearers knew this life pattern well! He is the keeper of Israel, who neither slumbers nor sleeps (Psalm 121:4; Psalm 80:1). He makes His sheep to lie down in green pastures and leads them beside the still waters (Psalm 23:2), feeding His flock like a shepherd (Isaiah 40:11; Psalm 79:13; Psalm 95:7; Ezekiel 34:14). Even in the valley where death casts its terrifying shadows, they need not fear, for He is with them, comforting them with His reassuring presence (Psalm 23:4).

Also: "I have gone astray like a lost sheep" (Psalm 119:176); "All we like sheep have gone astray; we have turned every one to his own way" (Isaiah 53:6a). Instead of punishing us, "The Lord has laid on Him the iniquity of us all. He was oppressed and He was afflicted" (53:6b–7). This prophetic passage finds its fulfillment in Jesus, the Good Shepherd, who "gives His life for the sheep" (John 10:11; 19:30). He restores those who have strayed away (1 Peter 2:25), carrying them home upon His shoulders rejoicing (Luke 15:5). He turns them over to undershepherds like Peter, and all Christian pastors and teachers since. With the commission, "Feed My lambs. ... Feed My sheep," He asks the searching question, "Do you love Me?" (John 21:15–17). As we become better acquainted with our Good Shepherd, study His Word, imitate His methods, and reflect on His unselfish love, He will help us find, bring in, and teach His lambs, until there will be "one fold and one Shepherd" (John 10:16).

Review Questions and Exercises

1. How was it an advantage for God's covenant people to live in Palestine instead of the Nile Delta or the Sinai Wilderness?
2. How does knowledge of the use of a sling help you better understand David's victory over Goliath?
3. What role did fishing play in the economy of the Sea of Galilee? What are some of the more popular types of fish in this sea? Which of Jesus' disciples were involved in the fishing industry? What types of fishing are reflected in the Gospels?
4. Why were sheep and goats such an intimate part of life in Palestine? Why is the answer to this question important for properly interpreting the parable of the lost sheep (Luke 15:1–7)?
5. How does Psalm 23 effectively portray God's role in our lives?

6. How does John 10:10–18 describe the role of a shepherd? How does this illustration describe Jesus' role as the Savior of the world?
7. What did Jesus expect Andrew and Peter to understand when He told them, "I will make you fishers of men" (Matthew 4:10)?

Chapter 2

Agriculture

At times tension and conflict developed between nomadic shepherds who lived in tents and the settled farmers who lived in the villages, surrounded by their cultivated fields. Beyond the fields lay the wilderness—rough country, too unproductive to yield to cultivation. This was open range for the shepherd, who would pasture wherever he pleased. However, the farmer's fields were not fenced, and the sheep and goats could raid the ripening crops of the farmer or trample them to ruin. A shepherd or cattle herder might become careless, and friction would develop between him and the farmers. Abraham and Job were great nomadic chieftains. (See Genesis 13:5–6 and Job 1:3.)

A hunter or the shepherd may wander from place to place, pitching his tent wherever he can find pasture and water. Abraham and the other patriarchs wandered this way in Canaan. A farmer, on the other hand, must have a plot of ground that will be his fixed home. He will be reluctant to do the hard work of plowing and sowing if he suspects that someone else will harvest his crop. He will not develop a real love for his particular plot of ground, nor will he try to improve it from year to year, if he knows that after his death it will pass out of his family forever. God wanted Israel to become a settled nation as quickly as possible after their wanderings in the Sinai Wilderness.

The Land

Size, topography, and climate of Palestine. Palestine was and is a small country. Dan in the north is only 150 miles from Beersheba in the south. Accho (Ptolemais, Acre today) on the Mediterranean is about 28 miles from the Sea of Galilee. From the Mediterranean shore at Gaza in the south to the Dead Sea is only 60 miles.

Palestine has a fertile coastal plain of varying width along the Mediterranean. Low hills next to it grow in height to almost 2,900 feet at Bethel and over 3,000 feet at Hebron. In the 65 miles from the Sea of Galilee to the Dead Sea the Jordan Valley descends from about 700 feet below sea level to almost 1,300 feet below sea level. The hills east of the Jordan rise steeply to well over a thousand feet. But in the hills we find fertile valleys and plains, especially west of the Jordan Valley. Many hill slopes are terraced, especially for growing grapes and various kinds of fruits. Lower Galilee and Samaria are especially fertile.

The climate of Palestine and other parts of the Near East is divided into the rainy and the dry season. Farmers hope for the first showers in the early part of October, but they may come later. The early rains are the plowing and sowing rains. The heavier rains usually come from December through the months of February into March. The late (latter) rains come in April, and the people hope at least a shower will come early in May before the rainy season ends. In ideal conditions the rains come at the *right* time, in the *right* way, and in the *right* amount.

The only moisture during the dry season is that of dew. It is formed by the west breezes and winds blowing off the Mediterranean. These usually begin in the late afternoon and continue into the evening. The negative winds are the east and the southeast winds that blow off the great Arabian Desert. The south winds blowing in from Negev and the wilderness of Sinai are also negative. One of these negative winds is the *chamzin,* which is normally dustladen and at times very humid. Worse is the *sirocco,* which can be extremely hot and destructive. In the morning the landscape may be beautifully green with flowers and by evening all may be burned to a crisp. At times the effect of this destructive wind is used as a picture of death (Psalm 103:15–16; Isaiah 40:6–8; Ezekiel 17:10; Hosea 13:15).

Palestine's condition at the time of Joshua. It required more than a few years, and more than a few generations of devoted farmers, to raise the hilly and at times rugged topography of Palestine to its highest productivity. The highly civilized Canaanites had been improving the land for generations during Israel's stay in Egypt and in the wilderness. In addition to the large areas of Palestine, which were extremely rich by nature, they had made many a steep hillside or barren crest into a "land flowing with milk and honey" (Exodus 3:8).

After the conquest the Israelites gradually took over this improved land. Joshua assigned a province to each tribe. Each household received a small portion of land that was to be the family inheritance forever (Joshua 13–14). Since the land was a prized possession, it was jealously guarded (Naboth's vineyard—1 Kings 21:3; "each man under his vine and his fig tree"—1 Kings 4:25; also Micah 4:4). The average Israelite may have received 5–10 acres on which to provide a living for his family. This estimate assumes a comparatively thin population for the more difficult hilly regions of the highland ridge, the barren sandhills of the south, and the dry grazing lands of the eastern plateau.

Landmarks showed the boundaries of the landowners on all sides. Details had to be specified—often trees, caves, or borders (Genesis 23:17—Machpelah; Hosea 5:10). Changing or removing a landmark has always been a major offense in Palestine. ("Cursed is the one who moves his neighbor's landmark"—Deuteronomy 27:17). It calls down God's curse. Job comments on this in Job 24:2.

Types of land; improvement by clearing and terracing. The soil of Palestine varied greatly. Fertile brown and black loam covered the costal plain and inland valleys. The most fertile were the Plain of Sharon, the Plain of Esdraelon, the plateau around Samaria, and the Jordan Valley. These are the "fruitful fields" of Scriptures (Isaiah 29:17; Isaiah 32:15–16). The hills and highlands were often barren soil. The wilderness was marked by drought, heat, and a lack of water (Zephaniah 2:13; Psalm 107:33–35; Exodus 3:18; Micah 1:4–13; 2 Corinthians 11:26).

The small family plot might include widely varying types

of soil. Here was a secluded valley which would yield rich crops at once. There an old Canaanite terrace wall had fallen down and needed immediate attention.

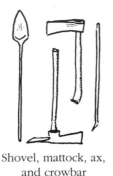

Shovel, mattock, ax, and crowbar

A terraced hillside

Perhaps a steep hillside, strewn with boulders and covered with underbrush, could be used only as pasture land for the sheep and goats, but it could gradually be made into excellent farm land. The farmer could clear away the bushes and weeds with shovel, ax, and mattock. One by one he could pick up or dig out the boulders. He and his sons, with the help of the oxen, could drag them down the hill a few yards and build them up into a strong retaining wall, roughly following the contour of the hillside. As time permitted, especially in winter, they could fill in behind the wall with earth until they had formed a section of level terrace. There next year they could plant a little more wheat or barley or vegetables. As more farm land was needed, more could be provided in the same way. Finally the whole hillside was covered with fertile level terraces. Farmers used no manure except that left by the animals in the field and the refuse from last year's crop.

In time thousands of acres of almost useless land, reclaimed from the erosive force of wind and water, were transformed into a "garden of the Lord" (Isaiah 51:3). Erosion could be very severe in the heavy rainy seasons. If the breeches were not taken care of, great damage would occur in a short time (Psalm 62:3; Ezekiel 13:10–14). Even houses could be destroyed by these undermining currents if built where a hillside torrent could get at their foundations (Luke 6:49; Matthew 7:26).

This development was backbreaking work. It required endless patience, perseverance, devotion, and faith. But where these qualities were needed, they were supplied. While the Israelites were gradually making new land, the land was making them. It gradually transformed those timid Egyptian slaves—those restless wanderers from the Sinai Wilderness—into proud home owners, passionate home lovers, patriots. Throughout her history as an independent nation, Israel's agricultural products were the mainstay of her national wealth. The rugged men of the soil, along with brave shepherds, were the backbone of her national defense.

The use of irrigation in Bible lands. Water is extremely important to both farmer and shepherd. The farmer cannot plow until the early rains soak the earth's surface. In summer while the fruit is ripening, fruit trees cannot grow successfully without irrigation. We do not know to what extent the Israelites used irrigation methods that they had learned in Egypt or that were in use in other neighboring countries. Irrigation machines did exist at that time. Unless a convenient stream or spring provided an abundance of water at a high enough level to flow into the gardens or fields, a device had to be used to raise the water from a well, cistern, spring, or river.

Cylinder irrigation device

In one irrigation machine a hollow wooden cylinder with an axle was set at an angle of about 30 degrees from the horizontal. Fixed to the inner side of the cylinder was a screw extending from end to end in a continuous spiral, like the conveyers used in grain elevators. Holding on to a convenient support with his hands, the gardener tramped up steps of wood attached to the cylinder. As he walked up the steps, the cylinder turned, and his body remained in the same position. The water entered the lower end of the cylinder and was forced upwards by the inner spiral until it poured in a steady stream from the upper ends into a trough that carried it where it was needed. The farmer could open or close the channel through which the water passed from one bed to another in his farm or truck garden. This was known as watering with his foot (Deuteronomy 11:10).

Cup-type irrigation machine

Another device contained a continuous row of pottery cups or jars fixed to an endless belt of tarred rope that passed over two grooved wheels. As the operator turned the upper wheel with a crank or— through an arrangement of wooden cogs—by the power of a donkey or ox, cup after cup passed upside down under the surface of water, went around the lower wheel, and came upright on the other side, full of water. As it approached the highest point on the upper wheel, it turned over gradually, pouring out its contents into a trough arranged to catch it. The "wheel, broken at the well" (Ecclesiastes 12:6) is a symbol of the termination of man's useful activity through death.

A third machine, used in the rivers of Persia and Syria, was a very large waterwheel, turned by the force of the stream itself. As the current revolved the wheel, cups of pottery or sacks of cloth, waterproofed with tar, carried the water to the topmost level of the wheel. There, as in the previous case, it spilled into a trough. In this way the ancient peoples raised large quantities of water to the storage tanks and aqueducts that supplied the people of the city with drinking water and those of the country with water for irrigation.

Plowing and Sowing

Primitive cultivation by hand. The processes of agriculture have always been largely determined by the power available to the farmer. Where the plot of land was small and manpower only was available, the people laboriously dug up the ground with a mattock. Even the comparatively poor, however, might have the use of at least a donkey or a cow, and yokes of oxen are mentioned throughout Scripture. Oxen appear to have been the usual draft animals, as donkeys and camels were the beasts of burden.

Harnessing animal power; the yoke. The harness of the oxen was very simple. The animals were fastened to each other by a yoke. This was hitched to the beam, or the tongue, of the agricultural implement. The yokes were of wood, constructed in various ways.

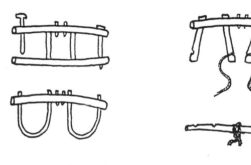

Square and round
yokes

Syrian and horn yokes

The *horn yoke* was simply a branch of a tree, perhaps five feet in length and from two to three inches in diameter. It was bound across the horns of two animals as they stood side by side. This type of yoke is common on the Egyptian monuments.

A *square yoke* was made of two horizontal beams fastened together in a way that provided two rectangular openings. The necks of the animals were confined in them by long pegs inserted vertically into holes at the ends of the beams.

Round yokes were made by bending green saplings into U-

35

shaped neckpieces and inserting the ends upward into holes in the yoke beam. They were bound fast or held in place by small horizontal pegs. The yoke was carefully shaped to the neck of the animal. If it irritated the flesh, pads of cloth or fiber were placed under it to ease the discomfort. A clumsy and poorly fitted yoke would severely hinder the work of the animal.

Likely the modern *Syrian yoke* was also used in ancient times. It has four flat pieces of wood, each about 20 inches long, projecting downward almost perpendicular to the beam. Thongs of hide or rope encircle the animal's neck.

Any of these yokes might be bound to the tug rope or to the tongue of the implement. They might also have a hole in the center through which the tongue of the implement was passed and then pegged or bound into place. Jesus says in Matthew 11:30: "My yoke is easy and My burden is light."

A yoke worked best if drawn by two animals as nearly alike as possible in strength or stature. A farmer tried to pair up his animals in this way. One Old Testament law reflects this: "You shall not plow with an ox and a donkey together" (Deuteronomy 22:10). In the New Testament the apostle warns: "Do not be unequally yoked together with unbelievers" (2 Corinthians 6:14). Not to keep in step would cause unbalanced walking. One walking faster than the other would tend to make an erratic furrow. Also, they might fall over each other's feet or one might walk right under the other.

The plow and goad. The Palestinian *plow* was a crude and extremely inefficient instrument. In its most primitive form it was probably cut from a naturally forked bough of a tree. One long branch formed the tongue, which could be attached to the yoke. Another branch, extending at a somewhat acute angle from the first, was cut off and sharpened to become the plowshare. Still another branch, extending in the opposite direction to the share, furnished a short handle by which the workman guided his plow. Plows of this kind were common throughout the ancient world and are still in use in primitive sections of the world.

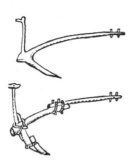

Palestinian plows

All ancient Palestinian plows seem to have been adaptations of the simple one described above. Because of the scarcity of good timber the draft beam was often made in two pieces, pegged and bound together. Pegs were set into the front end of the draft beam and a broad groove was cut at an angle near the opposite end to receive the plowshare beam and the handle, which were then tightly bound or clamped into place.

The plowshare was shod with a bronze and later an iron point. This plow was not much more efficient than the all-wooden instrument described above. Its plowshare was not designed to cut a furrow and turn it over. It simply tore up the ground in an irregular, haphazard way.

Because the plow was so light and shaky, the farmer had to wait until the early fall rains to plow his ground. He had to bend forward and put his weight on the handle to keep the share in the ground.

The plowman had to guide the plow with one hand and at the same time carefully press the plow down into the ground—a difficult task. This reminds us of Jesus' words, still valid in our work in the kingdom: "No one, having put his hand to the plow, and looking back, is fit for the kingdom of God" (Luke 9:62).

The plowman drove his oxen mostly with his voice. To keep his animals in motion or guide them to the left or right, he sometimes provided a gentle tap from a *goad,* a long pole with a chisel-shaped piece of bronze or iron at one end. This chisel end was designed to clean the mud from the plowshare, but it might also curb stubborn oxen. Jesus refers to this use when He tells Saul of Tarsus, "It is hard for you to kick against the goads" (Acts 9:5). Saul understood just what Jesus meant—

that he was acting like a stubborn ox. Shamgar used one of these goads, too, as an improvised spear to kill 600 Philistines (Judges 3:31). The plowman certainly knows better than the oxen which is the right way to go. So the Lord guides us, and we do well to heed His guidance and not kick against it. In Ecclesiastes 12:11 we are told, "The words of the wise are like goads." They move us around and guide us in our way.

Preparing the plowed land for sowing. After the plow had torn up the ground, the plowman walked along the rough furrows and broke up the lumps with a mattock of wood or of iron (Isaiah 28:24–25). He would also use a mattock or heavy hoe to chop up the soil of the sharper hillsides and little rocky spots where the plow would not penetrate, "And to any hill which could be dug with the hoe, you will not go there for fear of briers and thorns; but it will become a range for oxen and a place for sheep to roam" (Isaiah 7:25).

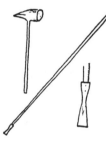

Wooden mattock,
ox goad, and chisel point
of a goad

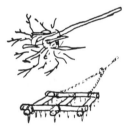

Brushwood harrow and
spike-toothed harrow

The farmer might then yoke his oxen to a harrow of brushwood and drive them back and forth to rake the ground fine. If he was particularly progressive, his harrow might consist of a wooden platform in which were set bits of iron or stone, or it might be a framework of beams into which long iron spikes had been driven. The preparation of the soil took place during the fall, beginning in October, immediately after the early rains had softened the hard-baked soil of summer.

Sowing the seed. Either immediately before the process

of plowing or immediately after the ground had been pre-pared, "a sower went out to sow" (Matthew 13:3). Carrying the grain in a basket, a sack, or a fold of his garment held between his left arm and his body, he walked back and forth across the field, scattering the seed with his right hand.

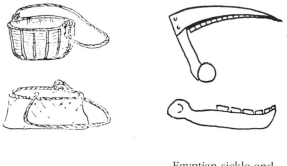

Ancient seed baskets

Egyptian sickle and
jawbone sickle

In spite of his painstaking care, some seed fell by the way-side and was trodden down (narrow pathways often went through the fields) and the birds of the air devoured it. Some fell in the shallow soil on the rock. Other seed fell among the thorns where the roots have remained alive or plants that already sprouted were not completely torn up by the plow. Most of it, of course, fell on the good ground. (See the para-ble of the four kinds of soil—Matthew 13:3–23; Mark 4:3–25; Luke 8:5–18.) Isaac reaped a hundredfold in Gerar (Genesis 26:12).

The sower was followed by the ox-drawn harrow or by a boy driving before him all the sheep and goats and calves. Their sharp hoofs trampled the seed into the ground. The job of sowing was done, and the seed was left to the processes of nature (the seed growing by itself—Mark 4:26–29).

Now came the rains. Intermittently the sun shone, and the grain quickly sprang up so that the fields were green by mid-November. Throughout the chilly months of December and January the grain remained fairly short, beginning to grow noticeably toward the end of March. When the heat and drought of late spring finally came, the seed head matured with surprising rapidity. The grain most commonly grown for human use was wheat. Barley served as food for the very poor and for animals. Other grains included millet, spelt, and vetch. (Older versions of the King James Version incorrectly translate *spelt* as *rye*.) The legumes included beans, lentils, and pulse.

Note the images in Isaiah 28:24–25: "Does the plowman keep plowing all day to sow? Does he keep turning his soil and breaking the clods? When he has leveled its surface, does he not sow the black cummin and scatter the cummin, plant the wheat in rows, the barley in the appointed place, and the spelt in its place?"

Cutting and Binding the Grain

Sickles used in cutting the grain. The time of harvesting varied somewhat with the topography of Palestine. It could come earlier in the lowlands than in the hilly sections. The barley harvest could begin as early as the end of April and continue into May. The wheat harvest normally extended from May into the month of June.

The Israelite farmer harvested his grain with a sickle. "Put in the sickle, for the harvest is ripe" (Joel 3:13). Early sickles seem to have been made of one half of the lower jawbone of a donkey or a cow. As the teeth became loosened, they were removed and replaced by small chisel-shaped pieces of flint, hammered into the tooth sockets, and caulked tightly with pitch or asphalt. The Egyptians made a sickle with a similar shape from wood and set with flints. Sickles of glazed pottery and flint have been unearthed in the ruins of ancient Canaanite cities.

Even as some used these more primitive instruments, others used more efficient sickles of bronze or iron set in wooden handles. These had many shapes and sizes, from almost straight knifelike blades to those with a crescent shape. Some had saw teeth toward the pointed end of the cutting edge. The Palestinians apparently did not have the large two-handed scythe or wooden-fingered cradle like those used in Europe and America for many years.

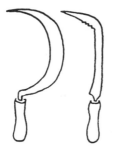

Bronze sickles

Wooden rake and sheaf of wheat

Gathering and binding the grain; the gleaners. The reaper cut the grain and laid it on the ground. Then other workers, called binders, raked it together, picked it up, and bound it into sheaves by means of a handful of its own straw. God's law forbade the binder to pick up what had fallen to the ground or had been missed when he gathered his armful of wheat. He must leave this for the poor gleaners, who, like Ruth the Moabitess (Ruth 2:2–3), came out to the harvest field to gather their scant rations for the coming year. "So she gleaned in the field until evening, and beat out what she had gleaned, and it was about an ephah of barley" (Ruth 2:17).

While the gleaners worked, a jar of water was available for them to quench their thirst (Ruth 2:9). At mealtime they might have a common dish of food that the owner of the field furnished them along with parched wheat and bread dipped in sour wine (Ruth 2:14). Corners of the field were left for the poor and the strangers (Leviticus 23:22). If a hungry person needed food, Deuteronomy 23:25 allowed, "When you come into your neighbor's standing grain, you may pluck the heads with your hand, but you shall not use a sickle on your neighbor's standing grain." This was true when Jesus' disciples plucked ears of wheat to eat on the Sabbath day (Matthew 12:1–2).

Darnel (tares), a sort of wild wheat, is hard to distinguish

41

from wheat until the spikelet heads begin to appear. Because their roots were often intertwined with those of wheat, the darnel could not be pulled out but had to be culled out. As the reapers cut the grain, they had to sort out the darnel a stalk at a time. These stalks would then be put on a pile and burned (Matthew 13:30).

Sometimes the ripening grains might be destroyed by a plague of locusts that were blown in from the deserts to the south and east (Exodus 10:13; Amos 7:1). Nomadic tribes of Bedouin horsemen often raided the harvest field or threshing floor (Judges 6:3–6).

Wooden cart with rack

Drying and transporting the sheaves to the threshing floor. When the grain was being harvested, the reaper cut a large handful at a time and dropped it on the ground. These did not need to be put into shocks, because the rains had ended. A rain at this time was considered miraculous (Jeremiah 5:14; Song of Solomon 2:11; Joel 2:3; 1 Kings 8:35). The bundles of grain were then hauled to the threshing floor and stacked up to dry thoroughly. It seems that a member of the family may have slept at night on its stack of bundles to make sure that nothing was removed by anyone.

Threshing and Winnowing

Preparing the threshing floor. On a convenient bare hilltop a circular plot of ground 30 or more feet in diameter was reserved for threshing purposes from year to year (Ruth 3:2; 1 Chronicles 21:15). From the time of the spring rains the ground was kept leveled and rolled until its surface resembled that of a modern clay tennis court. Some threshing floors used natural limestone rock, quarried smooth, with the crevices and depressions filled in with clay. The temple of Jerusalem was built on the threshing floor of Oran, bought by

David (1 Chronicles 21:18–30). Usually a low wall of stones set bounds to the actual threshing area. At times a series of 10 or more threshing floors were built side by side for the families of a whole village.

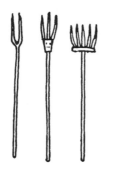

Wooden pitchforks

Threshing by means of cattle. At threshing time the bundles would be taken from the stack and spread as uniformly as possible over the threshing floor to the depth of about a foot. Sometimes cows, calves, sheep, and donkeys, driven around and around the floor, tramped the grain out of the straw and chaff. A row of cows or donkeys might be yoked together by a pole bound to their horns or necks. They would walk in one direction for a while, and then the other, to equalize the distance traveled by the various animals. The animals wore no muzzles, as they do on modern Arabian threshing floors. God had directed: "You shall not muzzle an ox while it treads out the grain" (Deuteronomy 25:4; 1 Corinthians 9:9). Sometimes the animals wore blinders over their eyes so that they would not become dizzy from the circular motion. Hosea says oxen were trained for the threshing and liked their work (Hosea 10:11).

Threshing machines drawn by cattle. Often a threshing sled might be used as a threshing machine. There were several types. One had a wooden platform, about three or four feet by six or seven feet, bent up slightly in front to enable it to slide easily over the straw. It was fitted with bits of hard stone or sharp teeth of iron on its bottom surface so that it might tear the straw and separate the grain from the seed heads. It was usually pulled by two oxen or cows. A man sat or stood on the board to weight it down; boys might ride with him to add weight and to have fun. Note Isaiah 41:15: "Behold, I will make you into a new threshing sledge with sharp teeth; you shall thresh the mountains and beat them small, and make the hills like chaff."

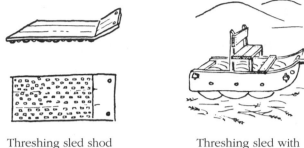

Threshing sled shod
with stones

Threshing sled with
disk wheels

Another threshing machine had a heavy frame with runners shaped like a sled mounted on three broad rollers. Each roller was fitted with three or four iron disks, forming 11 disk wheels in all. These wheels cut and ground and crushed the grain as a team of oxen dragged the machine about the threshing floor.

An Egyptian threshing device. The ancient Egyptians used another threshing device, which may also have been introduced into Palestine by the Israelites. It looked very much like a small diving board. It was firmly fixed in the ground at one end and sloped upward towards the free end at an angle of perhaps 20 degrees. Several rows of long wooden or metal spikes extended from the free end. The thresher swung a sheaf up over his head, and brought it down sharply so the head ends of the stalks were forced between the spikes. Then he pulled the sheaf upwards, stripping the ripe wheat out of the ear. The grain and chaff fell to the ground below the board, while the straw was thrown aside. The fundamental principle of this device was still used in the ordinary spiked-cylinder threshing machine of the 20th century.

The use of the flail. Sometimes the farmer chose to beat out the grain with a flail. A short wooden handle was bound to a narrow paddle-shaped board by a leather thong. Holding

Spiked threshing device
from Egypt

Wooden flail

the sheaf to the floor with one hand, the farmer beat the seed heads in a downward-outward motion until he had knocked out all the grain. Both the ingenuity of the farmer and the type of grain to be threshed determined which of the threshing instruments would best serve its purpose.

Winnowing and cleansing the grain. Whatever the mode of threshing, the process of winnowing—or separating the chaff and bits of straw from the wheat—remained practically uniform. The mixture was first shoveled and swept to the center of the threshing floor. Then the farmer took a long-handled broad wooden shovel or a close five- or seven-wooden pronged fork and threw the chaff and grain up into the wind. The chaff and lighter waste matter blew windward, while the wheat fell on a pile by itself. (See Psalm 1:4: "Are like the chaff which the wind drives away," and Matthew 3:12: "His winnowing fan is in His hand.")

Illustrations on the Egyptian monuments show men with two short flat boards about 6 inches by 14 inches with which they dug into the pile of grain and chaff and then threw it backwards over their heads into the wind. This chaff, comparatively worthless, was used for fuel or burned up in the fields. The straw served as bedding and food for the animals in winter. (See Isaiah 30:24: "The oxen and the young donkeys ... will eat cured fodder, which has been winnowed with the shovel and fan.")

Winnowing "fans"

After repeating the winnowing process several times, the farmer completed cleaning the grain. He used a sieve to take out the dirt, sand, and small seeds that might have escaped the winnowing process. (See Luke 22:31: "He may sift you as wheat," and Amos 9:9: "I will sift the house of Israel among all nations, as grain is sifted in a sieve. Yet not the smallest grain shall fall to the ground.") The farmer was very careful not to lose any grain in the sifting process.

A sieve might be a copper bowl punctured full of holes through which dust and dirt could fall. It might be a pillbox-shaped container whose open bottom is covered with a close-meshed screen formed by a network of linen or fiber threads or horsehair.

Measuring, Transportation and Storage of Grain

The measuring process. The measuring process was performed very carefully and ceremoniously with "good measure, pressed down, shaken together, and running over" (Luke 6:38; Mark 4:24). People in the East seem always to have plenty of time; in measuring it is worthwhile to take time. Up to 30 percent can be gained by careful measuring—full, pressed down, shaken together, and running over. This process appeals greatly to many easterners. If all measure this way, the end result is the same as if it were done by bushel measure or scale, as we do. The containers used for measuring were made of clay pottery, copper, or wood, in standard sizes convenient for handling. (See "Liquid and Dry Measure," chapter 7.)

Transportation and storage of grain. After the measuring process the farmer loaded the grain into sacks or baskets, slung them over the backs of his donkeys, and took them to his home. His wife carefully washed the grain intended for household use. She then spread it out to dry in the sun on

46

the flat roof or in the open courtyard (2 Samuel 17:19). She might sift it once more before finally storing it in large vermin-proof jars or in bins of sun-baked clay bonded together with straw or woven fiber, until the family needed it for food. (Note the jar of the widow of Zarephath—1 Kings 17:12.)

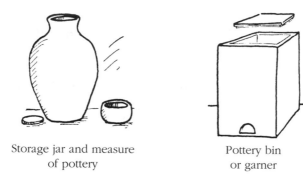

Storage jar and measure
of pottery

Pottery bin
or garner

Spiritual applications of the harvest processes. Like so many processes of everyday life, Scripture makes spiritual applications of the harvest. "The harvest is the end of the age; and the reapers are the angels" (Matthew 13:39). Again, John the Baptizer describes the Messiah as a thresher, giving his threshing floor its final, thorough cleanup of the season: "His winnowing fan is in His hand, and He will thoroughly purge His threshing floor, and gather His wheat into the barn; but He will burn up the chaff with unquenchable fire" (Matthew 3:12; Luke 3:17). Jesus looked upon humanity of His own day as "fields ... already white for harvest" (John 4:35). It is a task not for one but for many workers. To His disciples of all ages He says, "The harvest truly is plentiful, but the laborers are few. Therefore pray the Lord of the harvest to send out laborers into His harvest" (Matthew 9:37–38).

Review Questions and Exercises

1. Why was land ownership important for the Israelites to develop a settled and prosperous agriculture?
2. What were Palestine's main crops? Why were these so important?

3. Why was terracing a hillside important for life in Palestine? Make a diagram to illustrate your description.
4. How did the climate of Palestine affect farming and the growing of fruit?
5. Compare the ancient plow and its use with a plow in our age.
6. Outline the process of cutting grain with a diagram of the tools used. What was the purpose of gleaning a field? Who normally was permitted to do this?
7. Describe the process of separating the grain from the straw. How did the climate of Palestine influence the process? Why was this a striking illustration for Jesus to use as a description of what will happen on Judgment Day?

Additional Activities

1. Examine the parable of the four soils (Matthew 13:3–23; Mark 4:3–8; Luke 8:5–8). How and why is this parable important for a congregation and its members? Why is the proper understanding of the term *seed* important for this parable and its implications for a congregation?
2. John the Baptizer used a powerful description of the threshing process in Matthew 3:11–12 and Luke 3:15–18. Carefully explain the whole passage and its meaning for us.
3. How may the agricultural process be used as a model to picture the work of each member of the congregation in its mission? Carefully describe God's role in this (Mark 4:26–29). How much does He delegate to us?
4. Why was Palestine's location in the Near East so important for the history and role of God's covenant people? How is this reflected in the book of Acts?

Chapter 3

Vineyards
and Orchards

One can hardly overestimate the importance of fruit in Palestinian life. In fact, grapes and olives, along with grain, were the most important crops of Palestine. The words *wine, vine, vineyard, vintage,* and *grapes* are used so frequently in Scripture that they show the importance of this fruit to the total economy.

Climate and soil were ideal for their culture. While the rough nature of many hilly sections made it almost impossible to grow wheat or barley, a fig tree or two could take root and find nourishment. On the stony hillsides, too barren even for sheep and goats to find food, grew great networks of grapevines. They were firmly rooted in some pocket of rich soil that was hidden in a deep crevice of the forbidding limestone waste. In land too loose and sandy to insure a surface crop, the hardy and long-lived olive, striking its roots deep,

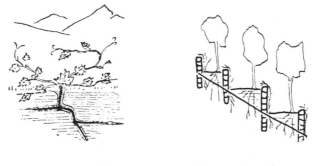

Grapevine rooted in
a crevice

Cross section of a terraced
vineyard

defied the blazing sun of summer through year after year of drought. Besides furnishing food and drink to the people of

Palestine itself, the vine and olive and other fruit trees supplied great quantities of their products for export. These were exchanged for copper, iron, precious stones, spices, ointments, and other commodities.

Building and Caring for the Vineyard

Reclaiming the hillsides and planting the vines. Grapevines grew wild in many sections of Palestine. However, the people were not satisfied with the wild variety or with the haphazard method in which they grew on the hillsides. Even at the time of the Hebrew conquest the land was covered with vineyards bearing clusters of grapes that amazed the spies sent by Moses (Numbers 13:23–27). The Israelites built up and expanded this industry. Their care of their vineyards is a symbol of God's care for Israel, His vineyard (Psalm 80:8–19; Isaiah 5:1–2).

As with agriculture, the hillside often had to be cleared of stones, which were dug up with hoes or mattocks. Thorns and thistles were taken out, and the hillside was then terraced so sufficient soil could be found to nourish a full stand of grapevines (Isaiah 5:1–2; Micah 1:6). The terraces often had stones at one side to keep soil from washing away. The best location was at the foot of the hillside. There the vines could get enough exposure to air and sunshine, and the ground that at times washed down the hill was richer and moister than anywhere else.

The choicest shoots were then planted. They were carefully pruned, cultivated, and trained along the ground or over the terrace wall in the vineyard or about the home (1 Kings 4:25; Hosea 2:12). Most vines today grow along the ground in the shade of their own leaves. In this way they would get the benefit of dew after the rain stopped early in May.

The care of the vineyard. After about three years the vines were allowed to bear fruit. With proper care and skillful pruning, they would produce for many years. The vineyard required more faithfulness and care by the farmer than any other process on his farm. Sometimes booths were constructed on the hillside. Four upright poles were covered with a network of twigs and leaves to protect the workers from the sun.

Watchtower and watchmen. A watchtower was usually built in the vineyard. A member of the family or a servant watched over the vineyard in the ripening period to make sure that none of the crop could be stolen. Isaiah 52:8 states: "Your watchmen shall lift up their voices, with their voices they shall sing together; for they shall see eye to eye when the Lord brings back Zion." So too a warning was passed along, as nothing escaped the eyes of so many. These are the towers or mizpahs mentioned in Scripture. They also served as fortresses to guard valuables and offer protection to the people in the vineyard.

In order to protect the vines from the "little foxes" (Song of Solomon 2:15) and other marauders, the vineyard might be fenced in with a wall six or seven feet high. It had a tall, often circular, watchtower of stone. The whole family might live there during the harvest. From the roof they could carefully observe the maturing crop in order to guard it against thieves. (See Isaiah 5:1–7 and Song of Solomon 2:15.)

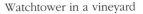

| Watchtower in a vineyard | Grape cluster and pruning knife | Ancient baskets |

Harvesting and Pressing the Grapes

The grape harvest. The grape harvest usually began sometime in August and went into September. The bunches of grapes were cut off with knives, gathered into large baskets, and taken at once on the backs of men or of donkeys to the winepress. There the juice was extracted before decay or fermentation set in.

The construction of the winepress. In the lower portion of the vineyard itself, or in the valley beneath, the owner "dug a winepress" (Matthew 21:33). Quarrying out of the solid rock if possible, he cut a vat. It was roughly square or circular in shape, around six to eight feet in diameter and from one to two feet in depth, similar to the familiar wading pools in many parks. From this shallow depression a number of channels led through the rock to one or more deeper trough-like containers quarried alongside, but at a lower level than the first.

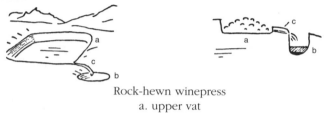

Rock-hewn winepress
a. upper vat
b. lower vat
c. channel

The use of the winepress. The men poured the grapes into the shallow upper basin to the depth of about a foot. They tramped around and around in the slippery mass until they had reduced the grapes to a pulp and the juice flowed freely through the channels to the lower vat. Here the seeds and other solid matter gradually settled to the bottom. One of the workers then dipped off the juice into large jars or directly into wineskins. He then loaded these into carts or on the backs of donkeys and transported them home.

The work of pressing grapes was, in itself, extremely tiring and disagreeable. The wine pressers trudged in the slippery pulp, holding to the branches of a convenient tree or to each other's hands to keep from falling. They lightened their burden by making a festival of the occasion. Handclapping, merry shouts, and song made the tramping easier. Accompanied by a piper who with inspiring music encouraged them to speed up their tempo, they literally danced about in the winepress.

Their quick steps made their tramping all the more effective. (See Judges 9:27, "they went out ... and gathered grapes from their vineyards and trod them, and made merry." Isaiah 16:10 prophesies, "Gladness is taken away, and joy from the plentiful field; in the vineyards there will be no singing, nor will there be shouting; no treaders will tread out wine in their presses; I have made their shouting cease.") During the rest periods the wine pressers refreshed their bodies with the fresh grape juice or with the wine of other years. Conversation, riddles, and jokes filled these moments.

This scene of enthusiasm and levity contrasts sharply with the prophetic picture of the suffering Savior in Gethsemane, saying, "I have trodden the winepress alone" (Isaiah 63:3). There is no one to help Him. He tramples, but no one pipes a tune to His solitary labors. He takes with Him Peter and James and John, but repeatedly they fall asleep when He needs them most. The anguish, the bloody sweat, the scourging, and the crucifixion must be endured—alone. Alone He works out the salvation of the world.

Sack-type winepress

Large storage jars for wine

Other methods of extracting the juice. Very likely other methods of pressing grapes were also used in ancient Palestine. The Egyptian monuments show a sack filled with grapes hung horizontally in an upright wooden frame. The workers inserted a stick through the end of the sack and gradually twisted the sack until they had wound it up tightly, thus expelling all the juice.

Modern Palestinians also extract the last of the juice from the solid matter in the winepress. They mix the pulp with clay until it forms a thick sticky mass. Then they heap it up, bind

53

it about with vines and fiber, and set a great flat stone upon the top of the pile. Upon this stone they exert additional pressure by throwing their own weight upon the end of a pole, hooked under a convenient rock, and resting upon the top of the stone. Very likely this method was also in use 2,000 years ago.

Wine and Other Grape Products

The process of making wine. In the home the wine was allowed to go through its first process of fermentation, which ordinarily began within a few days. After several weeks workers poured it off the lees, or sediment (Isaiah 25:6), and allowed it to ferment again. Then they might place it in large jars of stone and store it until needed.

More likely, however, they would use wineskins for this purpose. These are the "bottles" of the Bible. A wine bottle was made out of a goatskin, sewn together where it had been cut to remove it from the carcass. This formed a sack that could be tied at the neck and hung up. The resilience of the *new* rawhide took up whatever expansion might result from the process of fermentation. Of course, no one would think of putting "new wine into old wineskins," since the old dried and cracked skins from the previous year were unsafe (Matthew 9:17).

Goatskin wine "bottle"   Evaporation pan

Fresh grape juice and grape honey. God's people in Bible times liked to drink *fresh* grape juice in season. The hot climate and the lack of knowledge of fruit canning made it impossible to keep the juice in the fresh form for more than a few weeks. To preserve some of the fresh grape flavor, the housewife placed the juice in large flat pans over a slow fire and boiled it down until it resembled a thick syrup. This was known as *grape honey* or simply *honey*. Without any further processing, it was used throughout the year for sweetening, as a flavoring, and for the many confections prepared by the Israelites.

Some travelers have suggested that God meant this type of honey when He spoke of "a land flowing with milk and honey" (Exodus 3:8), but this interpretation seems unlikely. Regular honey was plentiful, especially in the wild and rocky sections of the country (Deuteronomy 32:13; Matthew 3:4). In the flower-covered Plain of Sharon bees were also domesticated.

Fresh grapes and raisins as food. Ripe grapes were eaten raw throughout the summer season. They had to be picked each day, especially if they were to be taken to the neighboring village market. Large blue grapes, similar to our Concord variety, were favorites (Genesis 49:11; Isaiah 5:2), but green, amber, and white ones also grew abundantly. As in the wheat harvest, passersby were allowed to pick fruit and eat it, but not to carry it away with them. "When you come into your neighbor's vineyard, you may eat your fill of grapes at your pleasure, but you shall not put any in your container" (Deuteronomy 23:24).

In order to preserve fruit for the long winter and spring season, bunches of grapes were made into raisins. Grapes were picked when not too ripe, dipped into a solution of lye to remove the waxy covering, dried on a flat rocky spot or on the clay housetops, dipped in olive oil, and drained again. While drying, they were sprinkled with olive oil and turned often to keep the skin soft. They were then left in the hot sun until thoroughly dehydrated. Raisins were stored in earthenware jugs or bins in the home. Rich in vitamins and minerals, raisins filled an important requirement of ancient Palestinian diet. (See 1 Samuel 25:18.)

The Olive and Olive Oil

The planting and care of olive trees. Olives, wheat, and grapes are the three important crops in Palestine. Olive trees, with their beautiful silver-green leaves glistening in the light as they were swayed by the breeze, flourished throughout Palestine in ancient times. Olives prefer a sandy, somewhat dry soil. They will thrive where many fruit trees cannot survive. Canaanites had cultivated the olive long before the conquest. When the Israelites under Joshua began to take over their inheritance, they found olive orchards already firmly established.

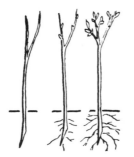

The growth of an olive shoot

A shoot from a cultivated olive tree may be planted, or olives may be grown from seed and grafted with fresh twigs from an older tree. Olive trees grow very slowly, requiring almost 30 years before they bear a full crop. However, they reach an extremely old age. By constant pruning and grafting, their period of productivity may be extended almost indefinitely. Olive trees in the garden of the Church of All Nations in Jerusalem along the Kidron Valley may have existed at the time of Christ.

In Romans 11:24 Paul speaks of people being grafted into His church: "For if you were cut out of the olive tree which is wild by nature, and were grafted contrary to nature into a good olive tree, how much more will these, who are the natural branches, be grafted into their own olive tree?"

Pruning was done with saws and pruning hooks. The pruning saw of the ancient East, with its pistol-grip wooden handle and curved blade, was very much like our own. The Lord tells His people to "beat … their spears into pruning hooks" (Isaiah 2:4), hooked knives at the end of wooden handles. These were used to cut off smaller branches with a downward pull of the handle.

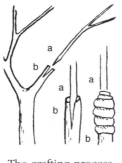

The grafting process
a. shoot
b. old branch

Pruning saw and
pruning hook

The olive harvest. The olive harvest begins in August, when the fruit is just beginning to take on a whitish hue but is still quite firm. Since the olives are still firmly attached to the tree at this stage and handpicking would take too long, they are knocked from the tree with sticks. A large cloth is laid under the tree. Olives for eating are handpicked or shaken off. Thus the Hebrew word for "picking" olives really means "knocking." This process damages the twigs and branches so much that the yield for the next year is spoiled. A farmer counts on a crop only every second year. Most of the trees bear in the same year, so years of plenty alternate with those of scarcity. Gathering the olives in baskets, the grower transports them, either slung across his own shoulders or on the back of a donkey, to the olive press.

As with wheat and grapes, God instructed the people to leave some olives for the poor. "When you beat your olive trees, you shall not go over the boughs again; it shall be for the stranger, the fatherless, and the widow" (Deuteronomy 24:20). "Yet gleaning grapes will be left in it, like the shaking of an olive tree, two or three olives at the top of the uppermost bough, four or five in its most fruitful branches, says the LORD God of Israel" (Isaiah 17:6).

Oil-pressing equipment. Many varieties of olive presses exist. The poorer people may simply use a somewhat concave face of the natural rock. A few olives at a time are placed into it and ground to a pulp with a stone held in the hand or rolled by hand over the fruit. Sometimes this process is carried on in the basin of the winepress.

The oil is extracted most efficiently in an olive mill. Olives are dumped into its basin. A large millstone fixed to a pole is rolled around and around upon them until they are completely crushed. Sometimes a camel or another animal, blindfolded, is attached to the pole and turns the stone as it walks around the olive mill. Several varieties of these mechanical mills are in use in Palestine, and the remains from ancient times show that the process in those days was very similar.

Ancient olive press

Grade of olive oil. Whatever the form of the press, the operation produced an almost immediate clean flow of oil, very light and transparent. This was separated and put aside as a first-grade product. Before long the continued crushing would add the brownish tinge of broken pits and the green of olive skins. The last oil to be extracted might be very dull in color. The owner commonly kept this oil for use by his own household, since the better grades brought higher prices on the market. The last of the pulp might be put into a sack and fixed into a wooden frame, where it received the final pressing to remove the last bit of oil. From the olive press the olive oil was taken in large pottery jars to the market or to the home.

Uses of olive oil. Perhaps no product was more indispensable to God's Old Testament people than olive oil. They used it in the ritual of consecration to the priesthood (Exodus 29:7) and the kingship (1 Samuel 16:13) as well as in the sacrifices (Numbers 28:28). It furnished the fuel for lamps and

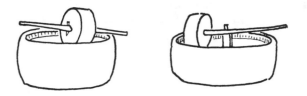

Ancient olive presses

torches (Exodus 27:20). People used it to anoint the head after a day in the burning heat (Psalm 23:5; Luke 7:46). After bathing they anointed their bodies with it. They put olive oil on their wounds as salve (Luke 10:34). In their bread, their pastry, and especially in their fried foods, it took the place of lard, butter, vegetable fats, and salad oils. The people depended upon it as a natural oil, food, ointment, medicine, and internal lubricant. As a result they may have spared themselves some of the digestive disturbances, bowel troubles, ulcers, and cancers that our modern age seems to have accepted as inevitable. As it was, plenty of sickness existed because of the woeful lack of disposal facilities for garbage and sewage, the swarms of flies, and the ever-present bacteria of the unsanitary Eastern community environment.

Shepherds and travelers carried olive oil in containers made from the hollow horns of animals, especially those of cattle and rams.

Horns of oil

The olive symbolized national prosperity (Psalm 52:8). Among all nations and at all times since the Flood it has been an emblem of peace. The olive leaf that the dove brought back to the ark (Genesis 8:11) showed that God's anger had abated and that He was once more at peace with the world.

Other Common Fruits

The fig tree. Various kinds of figs were also common in Palestine. They flourished everywhere, in the open vineyard or near the house. Times of peace and plenty were pictured as "each man under his vine and his fig tree" (1 Kings 4:25; Zechariah 3:10; Micah 4:4). When God "struck their vines also and their fig trees," there was hunger and despair throughout Israel. (See Psalm 105:33 and Jeremiah 5:17.)

Fig branch and fruit

As winter approaches, the fig tree sheds its leaves. It remains bare throughout the cold months. Rather late in spring the tips of the branches begin to thicken into globules. A few of these may ripen at the beginning of April (Matthew 21:18–19; Mark 11:12–14; Hosea 9:10). These are called the "early fruit" (Isaiah 28:4; Nahum 3:12). They are not as good as the later figs, but they are eagerly awaited and considered a special delicacy because they are out of season (Jeremiah 24:2; Hosea 9:10). Meanwhile the regular yield of figs is slowly forming on the green shoots that grew in spring. The summer fruit (Amos 8:1) is usually harvested in August and September.

Besides the early fruit and the regular crop of figs, occasionally there are also "winter figs," which ripen very late in fall. People look forward to them just as they do to the early fruit, because they too are out of season. With three crops of fruit, the fig tree bears nearly half of the time.

Leaves and fruit appear together on the fig tree, somewhat spectacularly, because they come after the other trees are green. They are, therefore, a sign that summer is near (Matthew 24:32). The fig tree, all leafed out, could be expected to have fruit. When one did not, Jesus cursed it as a hypocrite. Seeming to be what it was *not,* it did not have even *green* figs—"nothing but leaves." (See also Mark 11:13.)

Figs furnished a palatable and very nutritious fresh fruit over a long season of each year. When dried in the sun and packed away in pottery jars or in matted-together "cakes," figs were available for food the year round (1 Samuel 25:18). Palestine produced so many figs that they were exported to Western nations.

The prophet Amos mentions sycamore fruit (Amos 7:14). These figs are smaller and less tasty than the cultivated variety. They still grow wild along the highways just as they did when Zacchaeus climbed up into one of them (Luke 19:4).

The date palm. Date palms grew wild along the mild shore of the Mediterranean down towards the Egyptian border and in the tropical valley of the Jordan. Jericho, in the Jordan Valley, somewhat north of the Dead Sea, was known as the "City of Palm Trees." Palms also grew plentifully along the fringes of the wilderness wherever a moist spot or a spring of water made an oasis. The date palm was one of the most valuable trees of the Near East, particularly in the wilderness region (Exodus 15:27). Travelers have always depended upon this fruit, which they could pick and eat raw along the way. Like figs, dates were also dried and caked together for winter use.

The date palm

Palm trees are also found in Jerusalem. Branches were cut from palm trees and other trees along the way to give Jesus a royal welcome as He rode into Jerusalem on the first Palm Sunday (Matthew 21:8; Mark 11:8; John 12:13).

Pomegranates. The pomegranate tree is very much like our hawthorn, or "thorn apple," but taller. The fruit is larger than an average apple. It has a sweet, tangy juice and somewhat reddish-purple seeds. It seems always to have been a favorite fruit and is often mentioned in the Old Testament (Haggai 2:19; Deuteronomy 8:8; Joel 1:12). Spiced wine was made from its juice (Song of Solomon 8:2). A rich indigo dye, used for leather and cloth, is derived from its rind. Miniature pomegranates of blue, purple, and scarlet, alternating with golden bells, decorated the hem of the high priest's robe used in the tabernacle service in the wilderness (Exodus 28:33–34). Brass pomegranates adorned the pillars of Solomon's temple (2 Kings 25:17).

The pomegranate   Almonds

Apples or apricots, peaches, and citrus fruits. Apples are referred to in various passages (Proverbs 25:11; Joel 1:12; Song of Solomon 2:3, 5). Some botanists think that these passages refer rather to apricots. Apricots, peaches, oranges, and lemons flourish throughout the mild Mediterranean region. However, they are not mentioned in Scripture. Today Israel grows oranges extensively. Mulberry trees did not exist in ancient Palestine (wrongly translated in 2 Samuel 5:23–24 and 1 Chronicles 14:15). Today they are grown particularly as food for silkworms and sheep.

Nut trees. Almonds were among the very earliest trees to blossom in spring. They seem to have always been plentiful throughout the Near East (Genesis 43:11; Exodus 25:33; Ecclesiastes 12:5). They burst into bloom so suddenly as to be proverbial (Jeremiah 1:11). Walnuts are also common throughout Palestine. Shelled almonds and walnuts are mixed with dried raisins and figs and used at meals, and they are carried by shepherds and travelers for food along the way.

Apparently oak trees were very plentiful in Palestine. Rebekah's nurse was buried under an oak near Bethel (Genesis 35:8). Absalom caught his head in the thick boughs of a great oak (2 Samuel 18:9). The fallen people of God carried on their adulterous worship among the oaks of the high places (Hosea 4:13). Like the cedars of Lebanon, the oaks of Bashan were proverbial for their wood (Isaiah 2:13; Ezekiel 27:6).

"Husks" of the carob tree

Acorns from the oaks—and the pods, or "husks," of the carob tree with their bean-sized dark-brown seeds—still fatten the herds of pigs raised by the Gentile inhabitants of Palestine, just as they did in the days of the lost (prodigal) son and the unfortunate Gadarenes (Luke 15:16; 8:32).

Review Questions and Exercises

1. From Isaiah's description (5:1–7), show how a vineyard was developed. Why was this such an effective illustration for Isaiah's purpose? for today?
2. Why were olive trees so important for life in Palestine? Comment on the life pattern of olive trees.
3. How does the story of the fig tree (Matthew 21:19–22; Mark 11:12–14) help explain the growth of that fruit? Why were figs important for life in Palestine?
4. Where in Palestine are palm trees found? Why did palm branches play a symbolic role in the Palm Sunday event?

Additional Activities

1. Comment on the significance of Isaiah's prophecy, "I have trodden the winepress alone," for Jesus' work (Isaiah 63:1–6).
2. Why were dried fruits so important for the life and health of people in ancient times? Try to find out their food value.
3. Use clay to make a miniature olive-press.
4. Build a miniature vineyard watchtower.

Chapter 4

Food and Drink

According to Isaiah 3:1, bread and water are the "stock and store" (KJV: "stay and staff")—the two essentials without which God's people would perish.

"Bread and salt between them." When there is "bread and salt between them," two people have entered into an agreement of loyalty to each other, no matter what relationship may have previous existed. See Numbers 18:19 and 2 Chronicles 13:5 for examples of covenants of salt. Judas broke his relationship with Jesus by betraying Him after having eaten with Him for several years as His disciple.

After His resurrection Jesus ate with the disciples at least three times, not only as a sign that He was risen from the dead but as a token of His *renewal* of the *covenant* with them. No matter what has gone before, even Peter's denial, all is now wiped out. (See John 21:13–15.)

Water. The high ridge of Palestine is made up largely of limestone rock. Spongelike, its porous surface "drinks water from the rain of heaven" (Deuteronomy 11:11) during the wet winter seasons, building up a vast reservoir that makes possible "a land of brooks of water, of fountains and springs, that flow out of valleys and hills" (Deuteronomy 8:7). Sometimes the water gushes out "like a spring of water, whose waters do not fail" (Isaiah 58:11). In another place a well, dug deep, intercepts an underground stream, as at the famous Jacob's Well, where Jesus talked to the Samaritan woman (John 4:6).

Where people could not find natural springs or underground streams, they dug holes into the ground or rock. They created watertight containers by stopping the seams and cracks with pitch or by plastering the cistern wall from the inside. Then they directed rivulets of rain water into these cisterns from the hillsides. If the rains were not abundant or the cistern sprang a hidden leak and lost its contents by gradual seepage, their hopes were disappointed. The Lord, through Jeremiah, gives this familiar picture a spiritual interpretation when He says, "My people have committed two evils: they have forsaken Me, the fountain of living waters, and hewn themselves cisterns—broken cisterns that can hold no water" (Jeremiah 2:13).

In times of prolonged drought people had to "drink water by measure" (Ezekiel 4:16), and even the "nobles have sent their lads for water; they went to the cisterns and found no water. They returned with their vessels empty; they were ashamed and confounded" (Jeremiah 14:3). In the morning and in the cool of sunset the women of the village gathered at the spring or cistern with their juglike earthenware pitchers, which they carried home upon their heads or shoulders. For Solomon the "pitcher shattered at the fountain" symbolized death (Ecclesiastes 12:6).

A broken cistern

Cooling a jug of water

Modern travelers say that a supply of drinking water is always kept in a container standing in the breeze at the window, where it will be kept cool by evaporation of the moisture emanating from its porous earthenware walls. The sick or restless kept a small jar of water within easy reach at night, as did King Saul the night when David had him in his power and spared his life (1 Samuel 26:12–25). We see the importance of water in 2 Samuel 23:15, "David said with longing, 'Oh, that someone would give me a drink of the water from the well of Bethlehem, which is by the gate!'"

Bread. The other essential in the life of the ancient East is bread. "Lack of bread" (Amos 4:6) is a description of famine, a time when people "eat bread by weight" (Ezekiel 4:16), when "the young children ask for bread, but no one breaks it for them" (Lamentations 4:4). When hungry, the people wanted bread, not cooked vegetables or the broth of meat. Ezekiel pictures earthly prosperity by "fullness of food" (Ezekiel 16:49). Let us see how the Israelites prepared this most important food, bread.

Preparing the Flour

Grains used for flour. In the Holy Land wheat was the grain most commonly used for flour. While barley was sometimes eaten by the poor, it was regularly fed to the domestic animals. Spelt, millet, and even lentils were sometimes ground into flour as an emergency food. (See the strange ingredients of Ezekiel's symbolic bread, Ezekiel 4:9–17.)

Wheat, barley, spelt,
and millet

Stone flour grinder;
mortar and pestle

Primitive grinding devices. Perhaps the earliest flour mills were flat pieces of rock on which a handful of wheat at a time was placed. It was crushed and ground by a large stone held in the hand and rubbed back and forth over the kernels until they were reduced to flour. The grinder might kneel next to a flat-topped block of stone and vigorously push and pull a heavy piece of stone, shaped like a loaf of rye bread, back and forth over the grain. He used both hands with a vigorous motion like that of a woman at a scrubbing board. Such mills were used in ancient Egypt and may have been brought to Palestine by the Israelites at the time of the Exodus.

The Canaanite tribes still living in Palestine at the time of Saul and David used a rotary-type mill. The cone of the upper millstone fit into a depression in the lower millstone. The grain was ground by twisting the upper stone back and forth under pressure from the palm of the hand. The large mortar and pestle of stone, similar in shape to the small ones used until recently by druggists, did a fairly effective grinding job.

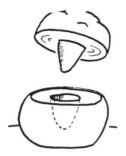

Canaanite mill

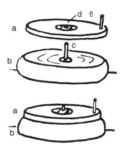

Rotary mill
a. upper stone
b. lower stone
c. axle
d. wooden bearing
e. handle

Construction of the rotary flour mill. Grinding was very hard work with all these devices. They required continuous pressure, with either a rubbing motion to and fro or a twisting back and forth. In most homes those grinding devices were replaced by the rotary mill, still in use in its simpler form all over the Near East and many other places in the world.

The rotary mill had two circular slabs of rock. One, the lower millstone, was about 20 to 24 inches in diameter and 4 inches thick, and often made of sandstone. The other, the upper millstone, was slightly smaller and lighter, and usually made of porous lava. Basalt was also used. The lower millstone might be set into the earthen floor of the home so that it could not twist and turn. A hole was bored in the exact center of its upper surface. A round wooden plug was tightly wedged into that hole. A round iron bar projected upward from this plug to form an axle of the upper stone. A four-inch hole was cut through the center of the upper stone. Across this a strong piece of wood was wedged without completely filling the hole in the stone. Finally, a hole was drilled into this wooden crosspiece, and the upper stone was slipped onto the axle fixed in the lower one. Near the outer edge of the upper stone a wooden peg protruded about six inches. It served as a handle with which to turn the stone.

The millstone could not be taken in pledge. It is "one's living" (Deuteronomy 24:6). Millstones today are likely much the same as they were in biblical days.

Operation of the rotary mill. The grinder turned the upper millstone with one hand, while she fed handful after handful of wheat into the central hole. As the wheat gradually worked its way downward, the rotary motion drew it outward between the stones, which crushed and ground it to pieces. Emerging as flour, it fell onto a mat or on the floor all around the millstone. To make the flour easier to gather, the lower millstone was sometimes fixed into a shallow pan of clay, reinforced with straw or other fiber. This pan caught the flour as it fell.

To lighten the burden of grinding, or for the sake of companionship, two women might grind at one mill, sitting crosslegged opposite each other. Each held the handle with one hand. They took turns conveying grain to the mill with the free hand, so that one could push while the other pulled the millstone around. Speaking to His disciples about Judgment Day, Jesus warns: "Two women will be grinding at the mill: one will be taken and the other left" (Matthew 24:41). Two women sitting close together, cooperating in a common task, chatting and friendly, are suddenly separated.

Grinding flour was usually considered a menial task, the work of the housewife or of a maidservant (Exodus 11:5). Note the insult heaped upon Samson when he, the imprisoned noted strong man, did the work of a weakling (Judges 16:21).

In times of famine there is no grinding, or the sound of grinding is low, for the grinders are few (Ecclesiastes 12:3–4). So Isaiah commands the virgin daughter of Babylon to come down from her throne to grind meal on the dust of the ground (47:1–2). John says of Babylon, "The sound of the millstone shall not be heard in you anymore" (Revelation 18:22).

Mill set in a clay pan; flour sieves

Sifting the flour. As it came from the mill, the flour was carefully sifted to remove the bits of stone and other foreign substances as well as the coarse particles of grain. The sieve might be a copper bowl punctured full of holes through which the flour could fall. A pillbox-shaped container might have its open bottom covered with a network of linen or fiber threads or horsehair that formed a close-meshed screen.

Making Bread and Other Baking

Preparing the dough. The grinding of flour, as well as the baking of bread, was usually a daily task ("our *daily* bread," Matthew 6:11) except on the Sabbath day.

To make the bread, the housewife used flour, yeast, salt, olive oil, and water or milk. She made a thick batter of the flour and liquid. She then added the previously soured yeast. She might make the yeast by adding a little sour milk to some flour and letting it stand in a warm place for several hours or overnight. Or a little dough, left from the previous baking, might serve to begin the souring process. The "leaven, which a woman took and hid in three measures of meal till it was all leavened" (Luke 13:21) illustrates the quiet yet effective working of the Word of God in human hearts.

Only at religious festivals, or when in great haste, did the Israelites eat unleavened bread (Exodus 12:39—the Passover;

Genesis 19:3—Lot). Its taste resembled the wafer used in our Communion services. The mixing trough was a deep pan of metal or pottery. Its size depended on the amount of dough to be mixed at a time. The consistency of the batter or dough varied according to the type of oven to be used in the baking process.

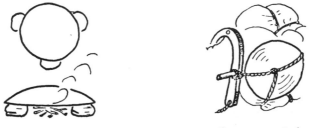

Simple camp oven

Camp oven tied
to camel pack

The simple camp oven. The simplest form of oven used in the camp or vineyard or on the road was a circular plaque of sheet iron, slightly convex, about 30 inches in diameter. It was greased with olive oil and held about eight or nine inches above the ground by three stones on which it rested. A quick fire of twigs, straw, or dried animal dung had heated the plaque. Then flour mixed with olive oil was baked into thin flat cakes of bread resembling waffles or pancakes, often as large as 20 inches in diameter. The resulting thin sheet of bread might then be broken into pieces.

When not in use, the camp oven could easily be stored away or tied to the pack of a donkey or camel. Perhaps Sarah used such an oven when she baked the bread for her heavenly visitors (Genesis 18:6). It is still standard equipment in the camps of the nomadic people of the Near East.

Ovens made of clay. Another type of oven consisted of a dome of clay, about three feet or more in diameter and perhaps half that height, built on the ground. It had a circular hole in the top, fitted with a stone lid. Small clean pebbles, scattered over the ground, formed the floor of the oven. The baker than made small roll-like loaves of leavened dough, allowed them to rise, and placed them on the pebbles. She then replaced the lid and heaped fuel over the whole dome. Under the hot ashes left from the bonfire, the dome and its contents reached the necessary temperature for slow, even baking. Then the baker raked away the ashes, took out the bread, put the lid back on, and covered the dome once more with the hot ashes to keep it warm for the next baking. Other families could then use the oven.

Mixing trough
for dough

Clay dome oven

Another common oven, still used in the Near East, was a cylindrical clay structure about three feet high and two feet in diameter, covered by a lid. When a hot fire had been built and then allowed to smolder, small loaves were stuck to the inside surface above the live coals. They were left there to bake thoroughly. Perhaps Jesus had one of these two stoves in mind when He said in Matthew 6:30, "Now if God so clothes the grass of the field, which today is, and tomorrow is thrown into the oven, will He not much more clothe you?"

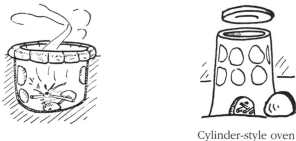

Oven in an earthen floor

Cylinder-style oven
of clay

A circular hole in the earthen floor of the home formed a stove in the living room of a simple household. Sometimes a thin sheet of bread was stuck onto the side and baked by the heat of the coals smoldering in the bottom—coals that remained from a hot fire that had been allowed to burn down. Several stones might be kept in the stove to retain heat for more efficient baking. Little loaves, or "cakes" of dough, might even be laid in the hot ashes or on the glowing coals themselves. (See 1 Kings 19:6 and John 21:9.)

Community ovens. According to the Greek and Roman custom, many of the people of Jesus' time may have baked their bread in very large ovens that served the whole village. Or they may have bought it ready-baked from one of the master bakers, guilds of whom were to be found in the larger cities throughout the Roman Empire. Women in some towns and villages yet today buy their flour and bake enough bread for several days.

Other baked goods; the use of honey. In addition to various types of bread, the women in Bible times baked many kinds of confections. These included tarts of dough, folded up from the four corners over a handful of dried fruit or a quantity of thick grape honey. Ordinary honey was taken from the wild bees, which were very plentiful in Palestine. The bees made their home in the rocks (Deuteronomy 32:13), especially in the wilderness of the Jordan, where John the Baptizer preached (Matthew 3:3–4). Honey in the comb was a delicacy (Psalm 19:10; Isaiah 7:15). People also extracted the honey and stored it in earthenware jugs (1 Kings 14:3). As to its use, Solomon advises, "My son, eat honey because it is good, and the honeycomb which is sweet to your taste" (Proverbs 24:13); but he also warns: "It is not good to eat *much* honey" (Proverbs 25:27).

Evidently people used honey chiefly as a sweetening in their various confections. They liked to make "cakes," more like our wafers or cookies, sweetened with honey, with which Moses compared the taste of the manna (Exodus 16:31). They had confections similar to our doughnuts, fried in deep boiling olive oil. Probably most other confections now baked in the Near East also existed in ancient times.

The Use of Vegetables and Herbs

Gardening with and without irrigation. In certain villages some people had a small plot of ground where they could grow some vegetables. Some may have been able to have larger plots. There they grew vegetables that they would put on sale at the village market. Some villages had market days on Mondays and Thursdays.

Wooden irrigation hoe from Egypt

Because the rainy season ended early in May, some irrigation was used where possible. Larger plots for vegetables might be arranged in depressed beds to make them accessible to an irrigation ditch. When this had been flooded, the gardener passed along the row of beds, opening up a passage into each with a hoe or his foot (Deuteronomy 11:10). When a row of beds was full of water, he closed the passages, one after the other, and moved on to the next row. Early vegetables did well without irrigation because of the moisture left in the soil by the spring rains. A second summer crop, however, flourished only where irrigation could be provided. (See chapter 2 for descriptions of irrigation devices.)

The legumes as food. Legumes, which are rich in protein and therefore a good hot-climate substitute for meat, were extensively grown by God's people in all periods of their history. Varieties of beans similar to our own were raised in large quantities. At maturity the stalks were pulled up, put on piles, and allowed to dry thoroughly. They might then be threshed in the same way as grain on the threshing floor. (See chapter 2.) More likely, however, the farmer beat them out with a flail. This had a handle and a paddle-shaped blade, bound together by a thong of leather. He then winnowed the beans from the pods and straw, sifted them, and picked out the dirt and pebbles. Taking them to his home in sacks or baskets, he spread them out on the housetop to dry very thoroughly. Then he

73

carefully packed them away in large earthenware jars or bins.

Lentils—legumes that look like small split peas—are reddish tan. Jacob used them to make a meal for Esau, who was willing to sell his birthright (Genesis 25:34). They were also a favorite and very nourishing ingredient of soups and stews. Black cummin, mentioned in Isaiah 28:25 and 28:27, has a round, black seed that is used chiefly as a flavoring material for stews.

Beans and lentils

Melons, gourd, and
cucumbers

Other common vegetables. Melons and cucumbers grew in both Egypt and Palestine, but not in the dry wilderness of Sinai. The wandering Israelites grumbled over their absence (Numbers 11:5). People used them much as we use them today. These items added substantially to the hot-weather diet. Wild gourds, though they smell like cucumbers, betray their poisonous nature by their bitter taste. A stew containing them was recognized by Elisha's disciples as "death in the pot" (2 Kings 4:38–41).

Onions, garlic, and leeks have always been favorites of the Israelites. According to easterners, they lose their strong taste when grown in extremely hot climates. Eaten raw with other foods, cooked by themselves, or used as flavoring in the main dish of the meal, they supplied important elements in the regular diet of the people. Parsley and celery were eaten raw or cooked with other foods (Numbers 11:5). Lettuce and a species of cabbage were also eaten raw. Dill, mustard, and coriander seed provided strong flavoring. Cassia, or cinnamon bark, yields an oil that was used for flavoring (Exodus 30:24). So do mint, anise (Matthew 23:23), and saffron (Song of Solomon 4:14), which was used to flavor both food and wine.

Potatoes, a mainstay for many people today, were not grown in the ancient world.

Vegetable stew. A favorite dish for the main meal of the day was a thick stew made of a combination of many vegetables. It might have a base of beans or lentils, with onions, garlic, celery, parsley, or other herbs and spices added. It might have lumps of dough, or dumplings, that helped to thicken it. It might contain small quantities of meat, fowl, or fish, which would thus be "stretched" to their full food and flavor value.

Dish of vegetable stew

The Oriental family meal differed greatly from our own. There was usually no table. Some had a low stool-like table raised a few inches from the floor, but people usually sat crossed-legged around a mat on which a large bowl was placed. Only the homes of the very wealthy had chairs and utensils of knives, forks, and spoons. Pieces of roasted meat were not cut, but were torn from the roast. Loaves of bread were broken into smaller pieces, which were then used to scoop up small pieces of meat and the thinner parts of the stew. The broth of the stew was sopped up with bread. A new piece of bread was taken each time. People would not put back into the dish bread that had touched the lips. A host who wished to honor one guest especially would scoop up choice bits of stew or a choice piece of meat and put it into the mouth of the honored person.

Dipping into the same dish was a sign of friendliness and mutual trust; refusal to do so was an insult. A betrayal of one

75

with whom one had dipped in the dish was the lowest form of unfaithfulness (Judas—Mark 14:20). John 13:26 mentions that Jesus gave Judas a morsel of the food before eating the main meal. After receiving it, Judas went out into the night.

After such a meal one needed to wash the hands. Water was poured from a pitcher over the outstretched hands. The surplus water fell into a basin on the floor. While usually the duty of a slave or servant, washing was sometimes performed for an especially honored guest by the host himself or by a student for his teacher. Elisha poured water over the hands of Elijah (2 Kings 3:11).

The Use of Meat

General economy in the use of meat. Good meat was scarce in Palestine in ancient times, as it still is today. When a farmer killed a cow, he lost both his source of milk and of power for his plow or threshing machine. If he killed a sheep or a goat, he lost his source of wool and milk. Unless he wished to provide a great feast, he would not kill the fatted calf, as did the father at the return of the lost son (Luke 15:23). The lamb without blemish had to be saved up until the time of the Passover Festival, when every morsel had to be eaten, even though several families had to go together to do it (Exodus 12:3–10). Except by drying meat in the hot sun, as was done in the Bashan cattle country, or packing it in salt or salt brine, farmers had no way to preserve it for more than a few days. Refrigeration, safe canning, and freezing methods did not exist.

Stewed meats. The use of small quantities of meat, fowl, or fish to flavor vegetable stew has been mentioned in the previous section. Meat might also be stewed in water in a pot over the fire, flavored to taste with various herbs and spices, perhaps with dumplings added. A calf or kid might be stewed or boiled in milk, but the Old Testament ordinances forbade boiling it in its own mother's milk (Exodus 23:19). Stewing provides comparatively large quantities of broth or gravy and also makes use of the nutritive value in the joints and mar-row. Therefore it is still a favorite way of preparing meat in the Near East.

Roasted meats. On very special occasions a calf, kid, or lamb might be served. This was done at religious festivals, particularly the Passover, when a long-absent relative returned home (the lost son—Luke 15:24), or when prominent guests (Abraham—Genesis 18:7) or a whole visiting tribe were to be entertained. A method similar to today's barbecuing was used. The animal was skinned and dressed, and the meat was seasoned and salted. A straight green pole, cut from a tree, was then arranged to pivot on two rocks or forked sticks at either side of an open fire. A pole was inserted next to the spine. The cook bound the sides of the carcass and its legs around the pole in a thickness as uniform as possible. The fire meanwhile had become a glowing bed of charcoal. Then the pole with the meat was arranged before the fire so that the drippings could be caught in a pan beneath. After several hours of roasting—until the meat was almost ready to fall off the bone—the meat was removed and cut or torn into pieces. The best pieces became the portion of various guests in the order of their importance socially or in the order of the honor the host wanted to bestow on them.

Roasting a kid whole   Roasting fish

Fish. Fresh fish were cut open and cleaned, seasoned, and roasted over the glowing coals of a wood fire (John 21:9–13) until they formed a crisp morsel. This could be held in the hand to be eaten (Mark 8:7). Fish might also be dried on the hot sands of the beach, salted, turned over and salted again and again, until thoroughly dehydrated. Dried fish could then be kept for some time without spoiling. At times they were ground into "fish flour." Travelers and shepherds could carry it in a pouch for their lunch.

Fish is an important hot-weather meat. The Hebrew people learned to love it as a food in Egypt. During their 40 years' stay in the wilderness they longed for the days when they had plenty (Numbers 11:5). Along the shores of the Mediterranean, along the Jordan River, and particularly near the Sea of Galilee—where many families made their living by fishing (Matthew 4:18–21)—fish were always available and inexpensive.

Fowl. In a country where meat was so scarce that two sparrows were sold for a copper coin (Matthew 10:29), and many other birds were allowed for food, except those specifically forbidden (Leviticus 11:13–19), it was natural that fowl would be domesticated.

Chickens are not mentioned in the Old Testament and only incidentally in the New. Jesus refers to a hen and her chickens (Matthew 23:37), and the crowing of a cock warns Peter in or near the courtyard of the high priest's palace (John 18:27). Chickens are mentioned often in the Jewish non-canonical books—the Talmud and the Apocrypha. They were raised extensively in the countries bordering the Holy Land, so it seems likely that they were raised in Palestine also. Various kinds of wild fowl were also plentiful throughout the region. The smaller birds included various types of doves. These were especially prized because of their fine flavor. The poor used them as substitutes for the usual lamb or kid in certain sacrifices (Luke 2:23–24). Fowl were prepared by roasting and stewing methods similar to those used to prepare meat and fish.

Eggs provided a good source of protein. Job speaks of the tastelessness of the egg white (Job 6:6). Isaiah mentions the gathering of eggs (Isaiah 10:14), and Jesus speaks of a son asking his father for an egg (Luke 11:12). No doubt the

Israelites used eggs just as extensively as did the neighboring people.

Ancient kitchen utensils

Milk and Milk Products

Source of the milk supply. A plentiful supply of milk typified the prosperity of ancient Canaan, the Land of Promise for God's people (Exodus 3:8). The shepherd out on the hills depended largely on the milk of his flock for his daily food. ("Who tends a flock and does not drink of the milk of the flock?"—1 Corinthians 9:7.) He used the milk of the sheep as well as that of the goats (Deuteronomy 32:14; Isaiah 7:21–22). Village families who could not have large flocks might still raise a few goats in order to have their own milk supply. People on the ranches of the East-Jordan Gilead and Bashan country practically lived on the milk of their herds of cattle, as nomadic peoples always have.

Families in the settled areas might have a cow or several sheep to provide milk (1 Samuel 6:7) and milk products for themselves and their neighbors. The cow might also do some of the heavy work. However, milk must have been scarce among city dwellers, particularly the poor.

Uses of milk. Fresh raw milk furnished an important item in the diet of the village family. It served as a beverage at meals (Genesis 18:8), especially for young children (Hebrews 5:12–13) and the sick. It was kept in jars immersed in cool springs of water or in the depths of limestone caves. Soured and thickened to the consistency of custard, it became a delicacy—and still is among people of the Near East. Commentators have suggested that Jael brought such soured milk to Sisera (Judges 5:25).

Cheese making. Soured milk can be made into cheese. The Israelites seem to have had many varieties. Palatable and delicious cottage cheese was most easily prepared. Dehydrated, in the form of tough curds, it found its way into the shepherd's lunch along with dried fruits and nuts.

Cottage cheese might also be pressed into lumps the size of a large ball, dropped into boiling water, and allowed to age. Such may have been the "ten cheeses" that Jesse sent with David when he went to see his brothers (1 Samuel 17:18). Many other varieties of homemade cheese, quickly made out of sour milk or aged through a number of processes, are still used in the Near East and in southeastern Europe, no doubt in much the same form as they were used in Bible times.

Goatskin churn

Butter making. Butter is mentioned in Genesis 18:8, where Abraham entertained God and two of His companions. It was made of cream, skimmed off the top of soured milk. The fat cells were broken down by rocking it back and forth on the knees in a jug or other container until the butter formed little lumps floating in the buttermilk. (Proverbs 30:33: "the churning of milk produces butter.") A device used by modern Arabs may be the same as that used nearly 4,000 years ago by Abraham. A goatskin "bottle" is made up in the same way as the wineskins mentioned in chapter 3. Half filled with sour cream, it was then inflated with air to make it comparatively rigid. It was suspended by the legs of the goatskin so that it could swing freely from a tripod support made of sticks. The housewife jerked it back and forth with a rope attached to the neck of the bottle until the agitation produced the butter. This method of preparing butter is, to say the least, unsavory. This goatskin churn is still used by Bedouins today.

Butter, boiled down to remove the water and impurities, was stored in jars and used in the preparation of baked goods, in frying, and for various other cooking purposes. We find no evidence that it was used on bread as we use it today. Buttermilk, the by-product of butter making, furnished a refreshing and nourishing drink for the family.

Importance of milk and milk products. In a country as hot as Palestine, particularly on the fringe of the wilderness, milk and milk products were vital to the life and health of the inhabitants as their chief supply of protein, calcium, and fat. Fresh milk, sour milk, and buttermilk provided a pleasant variety of refreshing beverages. Butter and the many varieties of cheese helped greatly in balancing and diversifying an otherwise limited diet. "A land flowing with milk ... " (Exodus 3:8) helped guarantee a physically strong and sturdy people.

Review Questions and Exercises
1. Why was a rotary mill more desirable than the earlier two methods of grinding grain to flour?
2. What is leaven? Compare it and its function with the yeast that is used today.
3. What legumes did the Israelites use for food? Which were used more than others? Why?
4. What are the ingredients used in a stew prepared by an Israelite household?
5. Why did the average Israelite household seldom have meat to eat?
6. Identify four ways milk was used. Describe the Eastern method of making butter, using a diagram if you can.
7. What kind of fowl were available to the Israelites for food? How was fowl prepared?

Additional Activities
1. Find as many similarities as you can between the action of leaven and the Word of God. Apply them to your own method of teaching.

2. Made a model of a rotary mill.
3. List the various kinds of food the average Israelite family may have had available during the four seasons of the year. Compare these with the food in your diet during the year.

Chapter 5

The Home
and Its Furnishings

No type of dwelling is confined to any period in the history of Bible people. The construction of the home, as well as the luxury or poverty of its furnishings, varied with its location, the climatic conditions, the availability of building materials, and the owner's occupation, wealth, and culture. Some houses served as dwelling places for many generations; others lasted only for a single season.

Primitive Homes

Caves. The limestone hilly ridge of Palestine is honeycombed with caves, large and small. From ancient times these served as homes of shepherds and their flocks. They became places of refuge for exiles such as Elijah (1 Kings 19:9), David and his band when they fled before Saul (1 Samuel 24:3), and the 100 prophets whom Governor Obadiah hid by 50s in a cave to protect them from death at the hands of Ahab and Jezebel (1 Kings 18:4). Caves provided shelter for the poor and outcasts and lepers. Often they were the last home of the dead (Genesis 25:9; 49:29). Some houses with a room on two levels were built against a cave in the stratified limestone. The animals of the family lived on the ground level, where cooking or baking was also done. The family itself lived on a terrace above the ground floor. Heating was not a problem in winter, since the caves remained at a moderate temperature all year. In winter the animal bodies provided additional warmth.

Booths of branches. A booth made of tree branches provided seasonal shelter. As a watchman's booth *on top of the tower in the vineyard,* it consisted of four upright poles connected by cross branches and covered with a network of twigs

A booth of branches

and leaves or grass to keep out the hot sun. A booth *near the threshing floor* might be such a framework covered with straw. The roofs were flat, since they were not intended to keep out rain, but the rays of the sun only. *At the Feast of Tabernacles* the whole nation traditionally moved out into such temporary homes in commemoration of the time when Israel dwelt in booths (Leviticus 23:42; Nehemiah 8:14).

Mud and reed huts. In the Valley of the Nile, and undoubtedly also in the tropical valley of the Jordan River, temporary dwellings were constructed of river reeds. These were woven basketlike to form the walls, which were then plastered inside and out with mud from the river's bank. The roof was covered with rushes. Although these houses were very flimsy, they served well the temporary purpose for which they were built. When such homes were swept away in the flood season of the Nile, the owner could easily build another hut.

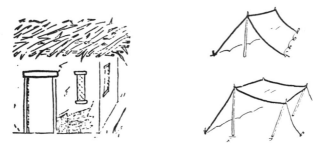

Woven reed hut plastered with mud

Small shelter tent

Kinds of tents. From the time of Jabal, who "was the father of those who dwell in tents and have livestock" (Genesis 4:20), nomadic people have lived in tents. These tents provided portable protection from the sun and wind-driven dust as well as from the cold of the desert night. Ancient tents seem to have been very much like those in use in the deserts of today. Tent cloth was usually woven from goat or camel hair. Tents made of goat hair were waterproof. The favorite color was black (Song of Solomon 1:5), in order to keep out the glare and reflection of the hot wilderness sun.

A lone traveler might pitch a small shelter tent no larger than a blanket to protect him from the sun by day and from the moon by night. Larger tents housed a whole family, and very large ones sheltered several families or a whole clan. The front wall of most tents was arranged so it could be held up on poles to form a porch roof or awning during pleasant weather. This could easily be lowered when a storm approached and pegged down securely to weather the blast. It could also be closed at night to shut out the cold. During their 40 years of wandering in the wilderness the Israelites lived in tents. Their portable house of worship was an elaborate tent in which God Himself deigned to dwell (Exodus 40:34).

Large Bedouin tent

The large tent and its furnishings. The usual tent of wilderness dwellers was very large, with at least two central poles. The roof sloped from the ridge to within three or four feet of the ground. It was held in place by cords (Jeremiah 10:20), tied to stakes (Isaiah 54:2) firmly driven into the ground with a wooden hammer. Jael drove such a tent pin through the temple of Sisera to rid Israel of the oppressor. Between the two central poles a strip of tent cloth divided the quarters of the men from the private quarters of the women. Household supplies and baggage were piled along this cloth partition.

Ancient lamps   A brazier

Inside a tent one might need a lamp even during the day. Lamps were made of pottery. Their shapes ranged from a simple shell-like dish with a pinched-in lip that held the wick to a very elaborate one, shaped like a teapot or a gravy bowl. A lamp could be set on a lampstand (Luke 8:16), or hung from one of the main tent poles. A cotton or linen wick, immersed in the olive oil within the container, stuck out of the spout and burned very much like the wick of a candle or kerosene lamp. Since no glass protected the flame, the light flickered and wavered with every breeze. When the oil ran low, the wick smoldered and sputtered. Isaiah uses this picture to illustrate God's mercy when he says, "Smoking flax He will not quench" (Isaiah 42:3; Matthew 12:20).

On the floor were woolen or goat's-hair mats and rugs of various sizes and texture, depending upon the wealth of the owner. Rolled up and stored along the edges of the tent, the blankets and other bedding served as couches by day. At night, with the rugs and mats, they provided beds. To prepare for bed the family removed only the outer garments and covered with sheets and quilts. The whole family slept on the floor. In a one-roomed house a floor would be almost covered by the sleepers. No wonder the householder tried to discourage his friend at midnight from making him get up to see him (Luke 11:7).

People were not allowed to take a small brazier for the charcoal fire and the millstone as a pledge (Deuteronomy 24:6). These—as well as the kneading trough (Exodus 12:34), the pots, pans, kettles, ladles, mixing spoons, and other cooking utensils as well as the bins, jars, and baskets of food—completed the essential inventory of the tent. This mass of useful material cluttered up the floor so that the young Saul could hide even his body "among the equipment" of the tent (1 Samuel 10:21–23).

The tabernacle shows some of these same features of construction. It too was rectangular, was covered with goat's hair cloth (Exodus 26:7–13), and was divided into two sections (the Holy Place and the Holy of Holies) by a curtain. The temple retains some of these same basic characteristics.

The Simple House

Building materials. The building material for the common home varied with the locality in which it was built. In the hilly sections of Palestine the houses were constructed of limestone rock or large stones picked up in the fields. These were bonded together with mortar that was made of lime, sand, and water. Along the Mediterranean, or in other sections of the country where rock was not so plentiful, homes were usually built of clay brick. This was true also in the

Wall construction showing cornerstone, lintel and sideposts, "head of the corner"

Tigris-Euphrates Valley and the ancient Plain of Shinar. There, in connection with the tower of Babel we are told, "They had brick for stone, and they had asphalt for mortar" (Genesis 11:3). Adobe houses, similar to those in the American Southwest, were built in the plains of Syria and Mesopotamia and the Nile Valley of Egypt.

Foundations and walls. Palestine has no sustained period of freezing weather. Therefore it was not necessary to dig down below the frost line. The builder merely chose a level site or leveled a site with shovel and mattock. Careful to place his building above the flood plain of a neighboring stream, he preferred to give it a solid footing on rock rather than on ground or sand (Matthew 7:24–27). He carefully measured out the size of the structure on the leveled ground, troweled a layer of plaster or clay where the walls were to be, and laid the stone into the soft mortar, carefully filling the spaces between the stones with mortar. At one corner he placed a large cornerstone (Isaiah 28:16); preferably square. This served as a guide by which he was able to find the place for the stones at the other corners. Then, using a stretched line to guide him, he laid stone after stone into a straight wall. He suspended a plumb bob from above to help him build a perfectly perpendicular wall. He fit each new stone in the same relationships to this line (Isaiah 28:16–17). Thus he laid up layer upon layer of stone, careful to avoid getting one joint exactly above another.

In the openings that formed the door and the windows, he built up squared masonry sides or inserted a window framework (sideposts, lintel, and sill) that he then built into the wall. Above the lintels (top stones—"headers"—of window frames) the wall continued for a few more layers. The builder laid four or five heavy roof beams across from wall to wall and built them into the masonry. Upon these beams, consisting of poles perhaps six inches in diameter, the structure of the roof itself rested. In the center of the house he might set a post on which to rest a heavy crossbeam to support the other beams.

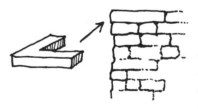

Head of corner

Head of corner. Whenever possible, the house was built on a stone foundation. A special stone was placed at the top of each corner. This stone was carefully selected and cut to be of equal length in each direction to firmly hold the corner walls together (see diagram). This stone is properly called "the head of the corner" rather than "cornerstone," which has a totally different meaning today.

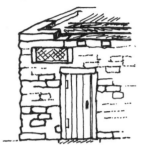

Door, latticed windows, and roof construction

Doors and windows. The door openings were about six feet high and perhaps two and one-half feet wide. They were closed with doors made of wooden beams or heavy planks and hinged so they would swing freely. The side beam of the door was extended several inches at the top and bottom to fit into the beam above the door and into the beam below the door to serve as the hinge of the door. The doors were held shut by a bar or bolt that slid into place. They might be opened or locked by a key inserted into a keyhole in the door or in the wall. Keys from the ancient world were very large compared with ours. They were made of wood or of iron and had a number of fingers or hooks that fit into openings in the bar (Song of Solomon 5:4). Doors of the more pretentious homes were made of heavy wood. They were studded with brass or iron nails or even covered over with a coating of sheet metal. In the finest homes and in palaces they might be made of solid slabs of stone with projections above and below on one side. These fit into depressions in the sill and in the lintel so the door could swing on these pivots.

Ancient keys

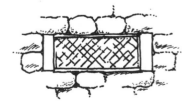

Latticework

To keep out possible robbers, windows were placed up high and were very narrow. Their openings might be left uncovered except for wooden bars and draperies arranged to cover the opening in cold or inclement weather and at night. Some windows were fitted with latticework of wooden slats set crisscross in a frame to fit the opening. While shutting out the vision of passersby, this arrangement enabled the people inside to get the advantage of the summer breeze.

Construction and use of the roof. Heavy beams laid across from one wall to the other formed the basic support for the roof. Smaller beams were arranged crosswise over the heavy beams. Other branches were laid across these, followed by a layer of rushes or straw. Next the builder shoveled wet clay in a thin layer over the straw and tramped it solid. More branches were laid in the clay, more straw, more clay, and then more rushes, continuously crisscrossing the material until the roof had reached a thickness of a foot or more. Now it was allowed to settle and dry out. Finally a very smooth layer of pure clay, like the finish of a tennis court, was carefully added to the depth of an inch or two, worked to a smooth finish, and left to bake in the sun.

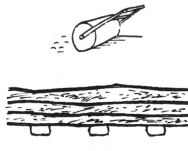

Roof roller;
cross section of roof

Such a roof needed constant care. After wet weather it had to be rolled with a small stone roller that was always left on the roof for that purpose. Depressions had to be filled in with clay, and leaks needed to be repaired at once, or the whole roof might cave in during a heavy rain, causing a deluge of water, mud, broken sticks, and straw to fall into the house.

The wall itself was continued above the roof line to form a short wall, or *parapet,* about three feet high. Either such a parapet or a solid rail had to surround the roof for the protection of those on it. In Deuteronomy 22:8 God commanded people to build a parapet to keep anyone from falling off the roof. The top of the parapet was finished with smooth clay and allowed to bake in the sun. Then the roof was ready to be occupied.

A stairway of stone or of brick, with carefully smoothed steps and a rail, was built from street level to roof line. Sometimes a stairway was built inside the house, emerging at one corner of the roof. There the walls extended upward, forming a penthouselike structure from which the family stepped out onto the roof.

When four men brought a paralytic to Jesus (Mark 2:4), they could not get close to Him because of the crowd of people around Him. So "they uncovered the roof where He was. And when they had broken through, they let down the bed on which the paralytic was lying."

Another type of roof used in the Near East today, and perhaps in the time of Jesus, has an arched or domed structure of stone that supports the weight of the clay above. Many pictures from the Near East show these domed roofs. Very likely they developed from the round arch and the cylindrical and domed construction of the Romans. Many modern houses do not have the parapet commanded by the Mosaic ordinances.

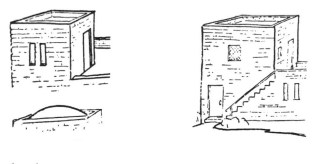

Enclosed stairway open-   Open stairway and
ing on roof; domed roof   upper room

The roof of the Palestinian home was very useful. It served as a quiet spot for rest and prayer because of its seclusion and privacy (Acts 10:9), a place to entertain visitors, to dry fruit and grain and flax and fuel, and to do other work (Joshua 2:6). In summer people often slept on the roof to benefit from the cool evening breezes. A roof was a very convenient extension of the house itself. So that they would be heard by those on the roofs as well as in the houses and streets below, heralds often spread their proclamations from this vantage point (Matthew 10:27).

Extra rooms. Some houses had an additional small room or two on the ground level. At times these were laid out separately. Each opened into the courtyard, which had a doorway entering into the street. One of these rooms might serve as a shop for the head of the household to carry on his trade as a carpenter, potter, weaver, and the like. (See chapter 6.)

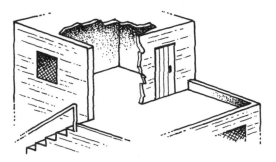

House with upper room

Simple houses usually had one room and were one story tall. An upper room might be built over part of the building by extending the outer walls upward and adding inner walls. These rested on supports beneath the roof that reached to the ground. Like the roof itself, a family might use this upper room for meditation and prayer or for rest. It might also be rented out for special occasions such as the Feast of the Passover or whenever crowds of people thronged into the city. In a large upper room, well-furnished, Jesus ate the Passover meal with His disciples at which He instituted the Lord's Supper (Mark 14:15; Luke 22:12). In such a room the disciples gathered for fear of the Jews after Jesus' ascension (Acts 1:13).

In villages the upper room might serve as a guest room

for visiting relatives or notables. Thus Elijah lived in such a room in the home of the widow of Zarephath (1 Kings 17:19). In order to have a place for Elisha to stay, the Shunammite woman begged her husband, "Let us make a small upper room on the wall; and let us put a bed for him there, and a table and a chair and a lampstand" (2 Kings 4:10). Faithful Dorcas' body was reverently laid in an upper chamber until the apostle Peter raised her from the dead (Acts 9:36–41).

Another kind of a house had a room with sort of a mezzanine floor running along one side, supported by posts on arches of stone. The family lived on the upper level. Sheep and goats together with a donkey or cow were kept on the ground level. In winter their body warmth helped to warm the house. Similar houses have been found built around a cave, in which the animals were kept on the lower level.

Furnishings of the Home

Utility in preference to beauty. A one-room house occupied for living, eating, and sleeping would almost certainly look cluttered. To the comparatively poor family, however, such crowding denoted wealth in this world's goods. Everything in the room served one or more useful purposes and was immediately available when needed. Beauty and symmetry gave way to utility. The house was a home and workshop for the family, not a showplace for visitors.

Mats, rugs, beds, and chairs. Mats and rugs, woven of wool, grass, straw, or other fiber, covered the floor by day.

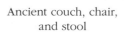

They also furnished a welcome protection against the cold, hard clay surface. The rugs and mats could be rolled up during the day and laid along the walls or stored with the bedding in convenient shelves or niches in the walls. At night they took the place of mattresses for the whole fam-

Ancient couch, chair, and stool

ily; the hard floor itself served as bedstead and springs. It was easy to get ready for bed. The mats and rugs on which a person reclined during the evening became the bed. One merely laid them out on the floor, pulled his cloak about him, and curled up for sleep. (Since the cloak was usually of wool and quite heavy, travelers or shepherds slept on the bare ground in the open air protected only by it.) Wealthy homes might have couches and beds. These had a framework of wood with legs about two feet long. A network of rawhide or cords stretched across the framework held a heavy mat or mattress.

Homes of wealthier people contained chairs and many kinds of stools. But in simple homes and in the nomads' tents, cushions of various sizes, or the mats themselves, took the place of chairs.

Stoves and braziers. In the center of the room stood the metal brazier or stove. It might be made of iron or of brass. Three legs were riveted to one or two circular hoops of metal so that a small fire could be built below and a pot or pan set on the upper hoop above the flames. For fuel people used straw, brushwood (thorn bushes—Isaiah 33:12), charcoal, or—more likely—dried animal dung, carefully picked up in the fields and stored in heaps outside the home for winter use. This fuel burns very much like charcoal with a clean, hot, almost smokeless flame.

Instead of a metal brazier, the stove might be a circular hole cut out of the solid earthen floor and lined with stones or plastered with clay, which then baked hard in the fire. Cooking utensils could be held over the fire by suspending them from a tripod or setting them on bars laid across the top of the hole.

Cooking utensils: ladle, spoon, pan, kettle, and basin

Cooking utensils. Cooking utensils closely resembled those used several centuries ago in more advanced civilizations and used more recently in more primitive civilizations. Pots of various sizes, hammered out of sheet copper or brass, were fitted with heavy metal handles so they could be hung over the fire. Pans of many shapes and sizes were also beaten out of copper. Long-handled copper ladles and spoons, as well as "flesh hooks," or forks, were used to stir the contents of the pots. Knives, made of bronze or iron in a variety of shapes and sizes, were fitted with wooden handles and served numerous purposes.

Many of the household utensils were clay pottery of simple rough texture or glazed by a second firing. Pottery jugs, with or without handles, served as containers for milk and water, olive oil and wine, as well as for the syrups made of grapes, figs, and dates. Many types of pitchers, cups, small deep saucers, and other kitchenware were made of glazed or unglazed pottery. In order to keep the dishes clean, they were carefully washed, wiped, and turned upside down to dry. (See 2 Kings 21:12.)

Solving the storage problem. Very large pottery jars or boxlike clay bins, holding up to three or four bushels, stored wheat to be ground into flour for family use. Somewhere on the floor there was room for the flour mill, an indispensable part of the equipment of every household. No one was allowed to take it in pledge, since the life of the family depended on it (Deuteronomy 24:6).

In such a crowded home, it is no wonder that the woman of the parable had to "light a lamp, sweep the house, and seek diligently" among the mats and rugs, the bins and utensils of all kinds, the fuel for the fire, and the dust of the earthen floor itself, until she found her lost piece of silver (Luke 15:8–10).

If the floor and walls were cluttered up almost beyond description, so was the ceiling. The crossbeams of the roof made convenient supports on which to hang "wineskin in smoke" (Psalm 119:83), in which the family's supply of this necessary beverage was stored. Large rings of onions and garlic, bunches of dried raisins, sheaves of dried dill and mint, and other aromatic herbs hung up out of the way, were still within instant reach when needed.

Herbs, onions, and "bottles in the smoke"

In this crowded home the housewife, poor or well-to-do, spent nearly all of her time. She took care of her children, prepared her meals, and did her spinning, weaving, sewing, and patching (Proverbs 31:10–31). Only during her daily chore of grinding flour outside her doorstep, or while enjoying her morning and evening trips to the village well to draw water for the family's use, would she get a chance to get outside and enjoy a chat with the other women of the village.

The home of Bible times was a closely knit family group where parents showed love to children, and children respected and obeyed the parents. This serves as a model for Christian homes of today.

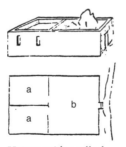

House with walled courtyard garden: (a) rooms, (b) court

Larger Houses

Homes with walled gardens. The simple house described above, or its expansion by the inclusion of an upper room or adjoining shop, was the usual home of the villager and the trade class of the villages and towns. The well-to-do demanded more pretentious homes. The rooms in some of these homes opened on a walled-in garden with kitchen vegetables and herbs, a few fruit trees, and a grapevine with its arbor or trellis. A balcony, reached by a stairway from the garden, led to rooms on the second story. You could enter the home only by one street door. The home was comparatively bare and forbidding on the outside, with windows narrow and high up in the walls. However, it was very pleasant on the inside with its fine view from all rooms into the landscaped central courtyard.

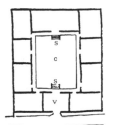

Floor plan of a house with central courtyard: (v) vestibule, (c) court, (s) steps

Homes built around a courtyard. Instead of mere walls surrounding the three sides of the garden space, a very large house might be built in the form of a hollow square. The garden space became a courtyard completely surrounded by rooms that opened onto it from all sides. In this case the courtyard itself might be slightly sunken. At times part of it was paved, and the rest was devoted to garden vegetables and fruit trees. Around the inside of the courtyard ran a porch, reached by several low stairways. On the porch level the doors led into the various rooms.

Because all rooms fronted inwards toward the spacious courtyard, large houses could be built tightly against each other on both sides and at the back, and right up against the street line in the front. They still would have an open sunny space within, with complete privacy for the family. Sometimes these houses had two or more stories. The porches, supported on posts, were reached by stairways extending upward from porch to porch. The flat roof over all the rooms could still be used in the same ways they were used in the simpler houses.

With houses so connected one could step over the parapets from roof to roof. Jesus advises His hearers to flee over the housetops of Jerusalem in order to escape from the city when the long-threatened destruction finally comes upon it (Mark 13:15).

Palaces of the nobles and priests. As the nation prospered, the wealthy and influential vied with each other in building mansions and palaces. The houses of David and Solomon served as patterns of luxury that later kings tried to exceed and that nobles and wealthier priests were quick to imitate (Isaiah 28:7–8). Spacious palaces of cut stone and marble (Amos 5:11), beamed with cedar overlaid with gold, were rightly viewed with alarm by the inspired Old Testament prophets. These were signs of worldliness, altogether incompatible with true devotion to the Lord (Amos 6:8–14; Hosea 4:6).

The outside of palatial homes in the city remained comparatively plain. Solidly built for protection, they had little ornament, except perhaps at the outer door itself. The door was the link between the dust, filth, and danger of the street and the warmth, security, and comforts within. Jesus uses this familiar picture when He gives to His disciples and then to His church the keys of the kingdom of heaven in order to admit believers to His own home (Matthew 16:19).

Built into these palaces were luxurious fountains and baths, patterned after those of Egypt and Babylonia and, in later Judea, after those of Greece and Rome. Couches of ivory (Amos 6:4), priceless rugs and draperies of the finest imported silk, and alabaster containers for precious ointments brought from the far corners of the world became the setting for the luxurious and rowdy parties and feasts put on by the wealthy Israelites (Isaiah 28:7). In such a home in New Testament times the rich man could clothe himself in purple and fine linen and feast sumptuously every day, scarcely conscious of poor Lazarus, who lay at his gate, full of sores and desiring to be fed with crumbs that fell from the rich man's table (Luke 16:19–21).

The homes of the wealthy, perhaps built with money gained at the expense of the poor and by devouring widows' houses (Isaiah 3:15; Matthew 23:14), often encroached on the property of poorer neighbors. Perhaps this enabled Annas, father-in-law to the reigning high priest, Caiaphas, to build a magnificent palace. Here the ugliest crime in human history, the murder of the Son of God, was planned and legally justified (John 18:13). Remains of such a palace have been found in the former wealthy part of Herodian Jerusalem.

Villages, Towns, and Cities

Haphazard grouping of homes. Instead of living by themselves on their own tracts of land, the farmers and shepherds of Palestine lived in villages. They did this partly for protection, but also because of the sociability of the people and their reluctance to be alone. In the morning the villagers went out to work in the fields and in the evening they returned home (Psalm 104:23). In harvest time, however, they sometimes slept at their threshing floor or vineyard where they had been working to protect their harvest (Ruth 3:1–4).

Villages and towns seem to have grown from one generation to another, often on a hill for protection. Walls were often added, also for protection. Villages were normally on a road and near a convenient spring or well. Though space was practically unlimited, the houses huddled together along the hillsides or in the valley, giving no evidence of group landscaping or street planning. The houses were crowded together so closely along a street that the roofs were continuous. Adjoining houses shared a wall.

Therefore it was possible to run along the rooftops and escape from the village without coming down into the narrow street where one might be captured by enemies. (See also Jesus' warning, Mark 13:15.) As the village grew into a town, the crowding and the need for straight streets and planned building became more and more evident.

An Oriental street

Streets and lanes. The streets were narrow and usually crooked. At times they followed an old trail along which the original houses had been built. Some of the streets were so narrow and winding that they were really lanes or narrow alleys (Luke 14:21). In the smaller towns and villages and in the poorer, unpaved sections of the cities they could become dusty in dry weather and muddy in the rainy season. To correct this problem, some were paved with stone. Here and there the streets appeared like canyons. Bare walls of houses stood like cliffs on either side or overhanging balconies almost met at times across the narrow space.

New towns upon the old. The houses were originally built with their floors a little above the street level. The inhabitants regularly threw out their refuse such as broken pottery, sweepings from the houses and roofs, as well as garbage and bones, to be picked through by the hungry dogs of the streets. This debris was tramped to pieces by the passersby, and much of it was washed away by the rain or blown away as dust. Yet the level of the streets gradually rose until it was above the average floor level. Then steps had to be built to lead down into the homes. By this time, however, if the house was of mud brick, it probably needed to be repaired or even rebuilt. Perhaps the roof beams or bonding materials had rotted and needed to be replaced. The owner might even level the walls to the ground so that he could begin building operations anew on the old site.

By now the debris and refuse of the wrecking process had filled in that site to a few feet above the street level. Thus, not only by the vicious destruction of their enemies, but also by the tearing down and rebuilding done by the inhabitants themselves, the level of ancient communities tended to become higher and higher. Some excavated communities are made up of half a dozen or more separate layers of dwellings. Each of these contains broken pottery, utensils, and other relics. Archaeologists carefully examining these items can determine the history of the various layers of the city.

Walls and gates. Many of the Palestinian towns were walled about with stone high enough to keep out the enemy. Some ancient walls were built of huge boulders, randomly

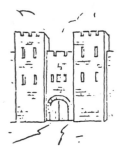

Walls, towers, and gates

laid up, and not joined together with mortar. Their own weight held them in position. That may have been true of the walls of ancient Jericho and the other strong fortresses of the Canaanites (Joshua 6). Other cities, especially since the time of David, were well-built masonry forts. Ordinarily enemies could take these only by a long process of starvation.

These strong walls contained a number of large openings or gates, through which the traffic of the main highways entered the city. The gates were closed at sunset and opened again at sunrise (Nehemiah 13:19). At either side of the gate, or directly above it, strong towers, with narrow slits of windows for the use of the watchmen, guarded the approaches to the city (2 Samuel 18:24–25). At the gate of the city, where he had been awaiting news, David mourned for his son Absalom (2 Samuel 18:33). The gates themselves were heavy wooden doors, studded with strong iron nailheads, or covered with metal for extra strength.

In Jerusalem the gates had various names associated with them. These were associated with the marketplaces within (Sheep Gate, Fish Gate—Nehemiah 3:1, 3). Jesus' reference to "a camel to go through the eye of a needle" in Mark 10:25 means exactly what Jesus said; He was not referring to a Jerusalem gate. The camel was the largest common animal. It was used to carry trade from many parts of the Orient and the Near East.

Marketplaces. Inhabitants might buy and sell in all of the streets of the villages. However, the business and trades of the larger cities tended to group themselves in certain streets and in special marketplaces (Acts 18:2; Jeremiah 37:21). On the market day sheep, calves, goats, vegetables, fruit, and fish (from the Sea of Galilee and the Mediterranean) were

101

offered for sale. Here, too, came the traveling merchants with their shiny brass utensils, the dyers with their bright wares, the money changers and tax collectors, the beggars and thieves, to ply their trade. The citizens came to buy, to window-shop, and to meet friends.

Here one found a cross section of the life of the community. It was a scene of noise and bustle and excitement. Wide-eyed children and curious strangers found something ever new and fascinating. Haggling over the price was and is an intimate part of life in the Near East.

Review Questions and Exercises

1. Describe a Bedouin tent—its makeup and furnishings.
2. Describe the house of the average Israelite—the materials used, the average size, the door, the windows, and the roof.
3. Describe the average small village in Palestine—desirable elements for location, houses, and streets.
4. Describe an upper room like that used by Jesus and His disciples at His last Passover (Luke 22:11–12).

Additional Activities

1. Prepare a model of a typical tent and its arrangement.
2. Build a model of a typical Palestinian house with a door, windows, and roof.
3. With the help of a good Bible dictionary or a good Bible atlas, study the layout of Jerusalem in the time of Jesus. Locate the Temple, the fortress of Antonia, the palace of Herod the Great (Praetorium), and the location of the Mount of Olives, Kidron Valley, Gethsemane, the Upper City, and the Valley of Hinnom.

Chapter 6

Trades Carried On in Home and Shop

In the Romanized cities of the Near East at the time of Jesus and Paul, the tradesmen had united to form guilds, or unions. Members had well-defined laws, duties, rights, and privileges.

Such trades tended to perpetuate themselves in families. The son followed the trade of his father and of his grandfather before him. People following the same trade generally lived on certain streets or in certain areas of the city. In this way they remained in close association with each other. At times they might band themselves together into pressure groups to protect their source of income, as happened in the case of Demetrius, the silversmith in Ephesus (Acts 19:24–41).

So it had been, too, in ancient Babylonia and Egypt. Here numerous tools used by tradesmen of a bygone age have been found, after being buried in the dry sand for 2,000 or 3,000 years or more. During the past 50–75 years many have been dug up and removed to museums. In addition to the actual remains, we have scenes from the various trades painted on the walls of ancient buildings or preserved in crude model form in the graves of great noblemen. We can see ancient relics, pictures, and wooden and clay models of animals and men, and of the tools they used. These, combined with the information in the Scriptures and in ancient literature generally, give us a rather complete impression of the shops, tools, and handiwork of the ancient craftsmen. Travelers in the East have found modern parallels to ancient descriptions. All these help us picture the work of the tradesmen in Bible times.

In Palestine, on the other hand, a trade was usually carried on right in the house of the villager, who might at times be also a farmer and a shepherd. He and his fellow citizens, as a group, made most of their own tools and implements, spun their own wool, wove their own cloth, molded and baked their own pottery, and tanned their own leather. All of these trades might be carried on in a fair-sized village. A family made a specialty of each for sale or barter to the people of the community and neighborhood in general. Work for a trade took up comparatively little space, since it involved mostly handwork. It could be done right in the home or in an adjoining shop, or even under an awning stretched over the doorway and along the wide front of the house.

The Weaving Trade

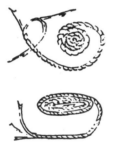 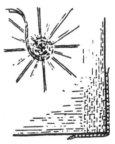

Braided-mat construction   Spiral and square weaving of mats

The weaving of mats. A number of different processes were used for weaving mats. The ancient remains show that the patterns, materials, and handiwork were very much like those of primitive civilizations today. In one process, strands of straw were braided together into a very long rope. It was then wound up in a close spiral and sewed into place with fiber until it had reached the desired diameter. By starting with a long line at the center, instead of beginning with a spiral, people could wind the rope into oblong mats. Other mats were made by laying straw or fine pliable rushes in small handfuls on the floor. Other strands of the same material were woven over and under and over and under the first strands from side to side. The edges then needed to be bound with straw to keep them from fraying.

The basic structure of another mat was formed by a dozen or so pieces of fiber, laid crossing each other at the center and radiating uniformly in all directions. Starting at the center, the weaver wove a long piece of fiber over and under the ribs in ever-widening circles until the mat had reached the desired size. He then folded the edges over and bound them all around to keep them from unraveling. By using straw or rush fiber, dyed in various bright colors alternating with the natural material, the weaver could obtain a great variety of patterns and color schemes.

Basket weaving   Ancient baskets

The weaving of baskets. The worker used the same method as that used in mat weaving to make soft, pliable baskets, similar to shopping bags. However, he pulled the material a little tighter each time he completed a circle. This gradually formed the basket into a hollow shape. He then wove or braided handles of the same material. He worked them through holes left below the rim of the basket on opposite sides. For strong and rigid baskets he used long, thin, pliable branches from willow, dogwood, or some other tree or shrub. Woven while the branches were fresh and green, either with or without the bark, these baskets dried into very strong and durable containers. Protective coverings with handles were woven around jars that were used for transporting liquids. Baskets of all shapes and sizes found many uses about the home, farm, and vineyard. They took the place of sacks, cartons, boxes, and other containers that we use today.

Spinning. When the freshly shorn wool came from the shepherd's flock, it needed to be carefully washed and combed, or carded. This process straightened out the fine hairs and removed snags and tangles. Then the spinner took a little tuft of wool and, beginning at one end, twisted it into yarn between her fingers. As she twisted, she pulled in other strands of hair, gradually, so that the yarn remained uniformly thick and strong as she went along. She could do her work more rapidly and uniformly by using a distaff, which held a large handful of unspun wool. She gradually drew out the wool into a strand of the required thickness. She let the distaff hang from the twisted yarn, keeping it spinning freely.

The distaff

Flax plant, seed heads, and flax comb

Though cultivation of cotton and flax was centered in ancient Egypt, Palestine grew great quantities of flax. Flax will thrive almost anywhere, very much like annual grasses and grains. From a small flat lozenge-shaped shiny brown seed, it grows a tall straight stem, ending in several tufts of seed heads and leaves.

When the seed is fully formed but not quite ripe, the flax is pulled up by the roots and bound into sheaves. These sheaves were taken to the housetops to dry in the sun. (Rahab hid Joshua's spies under such bundles of flax—Joshua 2:6.) Then the seeds are threshed out with a flail or stick. They are used as food for people and animals or are ground and pressed for the linseed oil they contain. To loosen the fiber from the pith and bark of the flax stem, the worker soaked the bundles of flax thoroughly for several hours or overnight. Then, handful by handful, he stripped them through the steel teeth of a brushlike flax comb. The waste fell away, and a thin strand of tough fibers remained in his hand. These fibers he spun into linen thread.

Cotton may not have been grown in Palestine in the biblical periods. However, it was grown in other parts of the Near East. When ready to be used, its seed heads burst open, revealing tufts of beautiful white cotton fiber. It was then combed and spun very much like the wool described above. For cotton, as well as for linen, a smaller distaff is needed in order to produce the finer threads.

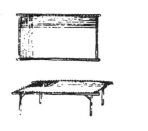

Looms for weaving cloth   Wooden shuttle

The weaving of cloth. Two instruments, the loom and the shuttle, may be used to weave the wool, cotton, or linen threads into cloth.

The loom is a framework of wooden slats or thin poles. Rectangular in shape, it can be set upright in a base so that the weavers can work at it from both sides. Or it can be placed horizontally on legs that hold it up at the desired height above the floor. Around the edges of the framework small nails or toothpicklike wooden pegs protrude from the frame. Beginning at one edge of the frame, the weaver ties the yarn to a peg. Then she passes it back and forth across the frame to corresponding pegs on either side until the whole framework is covered with parallel strands of yarn. A varied pattern may have an inch or two of one color, then of another, and so on.

Now the shuttle comes into play. It is a small wooden or bone instrument, consisting of two smooth flat pointed pieces fastened together by a peg as illustrated. On the connecting peg the weaver winds the yarn that is to be used for the cross weaving. She how pushes the shuttle between the stretched strands of yarn, above and below, alternating across the full width of the loom. She returns in the same way, thus going back and forth. Here, too, she may vary the pattern by alternately using shuttles wound with different colors of yarn.

Dyeing and bleaching. The people of Palestine have always loved contrasting colors—perhaps black and white or purple, yellow, and red in patterns of checks and stripes. As a result of this love for color in clothing, the ancient dyer did a good business. Vats were set in the pavement, like wading pools. He might make some of his own dyes from the bark of trees or roots or herbs. More likely he would import it from the East or from the great dyeworks of the Phoenician coast.

The very expensive purple dye was made from the very small amount of liquid in the murex shell found in the Eastern Mediterranean. Extensive amounts of these shells have been found in the harbor areas of the southern coastal plain of Palestine as well as of Phoenicia. A cheaper vegetable purple dye was made from roots of the madder plant found in the area of Thyatira south of Pergamum in the Roman province of Asia (modern Turkey). Lydia was the trade representative of this highly desirable, cheaper dye to the Roman citizens in Philippi (Acts 16:24).

Murex shell

Another favorite color, *crimson,* was derived from an insect that lived in a kind of oak tree or was made from a type of nut. The rind of the pomegranate was the source of *indigo*. Scarlet, purple, blue, and green were often placed side by side (Exodus 26:1). Many people in Palestine still wear bright colors, yet, relieved by grays, olive, lavender, pink, and fuchsia.

Dyed materials are allowed to pass through cold running water a few minutes after being in the dye solution for the required time. This tends to fix the color. They are then dried out. (This dyeing process refers to leather, but may also be applied to cloth. See "Curing and Tanning the Hides" in this chapter.)

Modern dyes have many colors. In the Arab crowd one sees bright crimson, powder blue, white, canary yellow, and indigo, in addition to Moslem green—varying yet always similar in the bright sun.

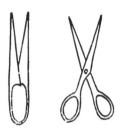

Shears and scissors

To get the desired brilliance in white cloth, the fuller (the one who finished the cloth) soaked the thread or yarn or the finished material in a vat of clean clay paste, or "fuller's earth." He then stretched it out in the hot sun to bleach. When the material had dried, he washed it thoroughly in clear water and dried it again, ready for use. At the transfiguration of Jesus His raiment became white, "exceedingly white, like snow, such as no launderer on earth can whiten them" (Mark 9:3).

The Carpenter

Jesus, the carpenter's son. We have a special interest in the trade of the carpenter because Jesus was a carpenter's son (Matthew 13:55). Since He began His ministry at the age of 30, Jesus probably spent His early years working as a carpenter. He may have used this trade to help support His mother after the death of Joseph.

The carpenter's shop and its equipment. Archaeologists have not found an ancient Palestinian carpenter shop intact, but they have unearthed many individual tools of various periods. These, together with the pictures of shops and tools from ancient Egypt and Babylonia, give us some idea of what a carpenter shop and its equipment looked like, especially as we compare them with tools now being used in the Near East.

The carpenter needed a space in which to do his work. This might be in a room of his house or in the street under an awning. It appears that the carpenter's bench came into use in Palestine much later than the biblical period. Ancient Egyptian monuments show a sawing post set into the earthen floor of the shop. To this the carpenter tied the beam that he wished to rip lengthwise. He then stood upright as he sawed. Perhaps this method was used in Palestine.

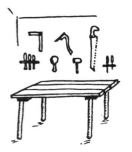

Carpenter's equipment

Ancient sawing post

Tools of the carpenter. The carpenter's saw (Isaiah 10:15)—a thin blade of bronze or iron—had teeth cut into one edge. We do not know whether or not these teeth were set by bending one tooth in one direction, the next in the opposite direction, the third in the first direction and so on, so that the saw would not bind in the wood. Some saws that have been discovered are thicker at the cutting edge than at the upper edge. The cut, then, would be wider than the thinner part of the blade. This would eliminate binding. The saw had a wooden handle into which the blade was inserted and then riveted into place.

Carpenters used two similar chopping tools, the ax (Jere-

110

miah 10:3; Isaiah 10:15; Matthew 3:10; Luke 3:9) and the adze, for smoothing off wood. They also used iron or bronze chisels, with or without wooden handles. Variously shaped hammers of stone and iron were fitted with wooden handles, similar to those of today. The carpenter used these to drive nails of bronze or iron as he does today (Jeremiah 10:4; Psalm 74:6).

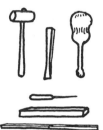

Hammer, chisel,
mallet, awl,
smoothing block, and
cubit measure

Adze and ax

Mallets—made of a knotty piece of wood—or other wooden hammers were used with the chisel to chip out holes or grooves in the wood. The rough-sawed or adzed surface of the wood could also be smoothed with the chisel or with a straight square block of limestone, which was rubbed back and forth across the surface. A metal-bladed plane may have come into use in Palestine by the time of Jesus, since the Romans began to use such instruments about this time. The awl (Exodus 21:6; Deuteronomy 15:17) was useful for making small holes in the wood for starting the drill point, and for scratching marks on the wood.

The carpenter's drill worked very much like an Indian fire bow. A curved piece of wood, about two feet long, had a bowstring that was wound once around a shaft of wood into which the drill point was fixed. The carpenter set the point in the desired place, held the shaft upright under the pressure of a block of wood held in his left hand. He worked

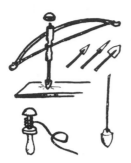

Bow drill, drill bits, chalk line, and plummet

the bow back and forth with his right hand, thus spinning the shaft with its sharp drill point. Drill points were interchangeable according to the size of the holes to be drilled. The process was slow and tedious—but effective.

Isaiah 44:13 mentions four instruments used by the carpenter: "The craftsman stretches out his rule, he marks one out with chalk; he fashions it with a plane, he marks it out with the compass ... ." The rule was a measuring line. Some suggest that this was done with a stylus. The compass may have been an instrument for making a circle.

The plumb line, or plummet (Isaiah 28:17), was a line with a weight (*plumb bob*) at one end. This was used to determine a line perpendicular to the earth. It was as useful to the ancient carpenter as it is to builders of today (Amos 7:7–8; Zechariah 4:10). For marking short lines as well as for measuring, the carpenter had his rules of wood in various lengths, marked off in fingers (or digits), palms, spans, half cubits, and cubits. (See chapter 7, "Lineal Measurement.")

Products of the carpenter's shop. The carpenter of Jesus' day was not primarily a housebuilder or skilled cabinetmaker. He was a maker of plows and yokes and other agricultural machinery, of ladders, doorways, doors, and latticework for the house, and of furniture and wooden utensils useful in the home. The scarcity of good timber severely handicapped the Palestinian carpenter as he competed with his fellow tradesmen in countries where good wood was plentiful. When David built his grand palace, and when Solomon built the temple, carpenters skilled in fine woodworking had to be brought in from heavily timbered Phoenicia, where the carpenter's trade had reached its highest perfection (2 Samuel 5:11; 1 Kings 5:2–18).

Wood carving. Some of the carpenters became very efficient in the use of tools, particularly of knives and carving chisels. The fine goldwork in the temple and in other elaborate buildings of the period of the kingdom usually had a finely carved wooden base. Thin sheets of gold were hammered into place over them, thus giving the appearance of solid gold.

There seems to have been a great deal of overlap between the trades of carpenter and wood carver. A good craftsman would be skilled at both. He made a living at whatever work was available.

The Potter and Brick Maker

Importance of the industry and source of materials. Ancient peoples needed *weapons* and *tools* to get food, and *vessels* to store it and serve it. Pottery filled much of this need. We have already noted the importance of pottery in the home. The potter's trade has always flourished in Palestine, since there has always been a good supply of clay and a reliable domestic market for the finished product. *Varieties* of pottery depend on the available clay and whatever color the potter adds. Each locality tends to make pottery of one distinctive color—red, black, buff-pink, or gray. The potters of Hebron were outstanding in this field.

Every housewife needed large jugs for carrying water from the spring (Genesis 24:13–14; Ecclesiastes 12:6) and for numerous storage purposes in the home (1 Kings 17:12). Many of her bowls, cups, and other dishes were made of pottery, which was quite fragile and often had to be replaced. Pottery could not easily be patched, but it was so cheap that this was not necessary. When God wanted to bring Israel to her knees, He compared her worth in His sight to that of earthen pitchers (Lamentations 4:2). To describe his utter worthlessness, the psalmist compares himself to a broken vessel (Psalm 31:13).

In a place where there was a good clay deposit, the potter shoveled off an area of topsoil down to the layer of pure clay. Then he dug a little depression into the clay itself, filled it with water, and tramped in it with his bare feet to reduce it to the consistency of mud. He then shoveled it from the depression, as fast as it was mixed, to a pile where the water could drain off. In baskets on the back of a donkey or in a cart drawn by donkeys or oxen, he took it to his nearby pottery. He kept it in pits to keep it moist and in condition for use on the wheel. The potter's clay was dug from a *potter's field.* As the last of the clay was removed, the resulting pit was used as the village dump. Here the people threw their broken pottery, stones from the fields, and refuse from the houses, including broken dishes and other useless articles. No longer useful for agriculture or for any other purpose, it finally was fit only as a burial ground for the poor and for unknown strangers. Thus we find the Jewish leaders buying a potter's field with the money Judas had earned by betraying Jesus (Matthew 27:3–7). (This area had good clay. En-rogel, a spring nearby in the Kidron Valley, was a source of water for the potter. It lay near the junction of the Hinnom and Tyropoean Valleys.)

How pottery was formed. Pottery may be roughly shaped by hand from puttylike clay, without the aid of any mechanical device, as many primitive nations still make it. Some of the ancient Palestinian pottery was made in this way. Very early, however, the invention of various types of the potter's wheel sped up and greatly improved the process.

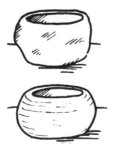

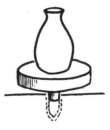

Hand-shaped and
wheel-molded pottery

Simple potter's wheel

114

A very simple potter's wheel consisted of an upright shaft of wood set in a socket of stone fixed in the floor so that it could rotate easily. A "wheel" very similar to the seat of a revolving piano stool was fastened on the top. In its simplest form the potter twirled the wheel with one hand or with the sole of his foot while sitting cross-legged on the floor in front of it.

A more developed form uses the same principle but has a longer shaft. A larger and heavier wheel is mounted near the bottom. This is then built into a worktable so that the upper wheel is just above the level of the table and the lower wheel is near the floor. The operator is able to sit on a bench next to the worktable and rest his weight on one foot. He keeps the wheel in motion with the other. Palestinian potters use this type of wheel today, and their forefathers may well have used it two or three thousand years ago.

Potter's table with wheel built in

Whatever the type of wheel, the operator kneads or treads the lump of clay to puttylike consistency and then flattens it out on the wheel somewhat like a very thick pancake. He then rotates his wheel, forming the clay with his hands with an outward-upward pressure as it spins, until he has shaped the bottom and the beginnings of the side wall as he wants them. By this time his clay supply may be exhausted, so he stops the wheel and adds another lump. This time he arranges it in the form of a snake and lays it along the upper rim of the partly formed pot. Rotating the wheel again, he rubs and pushes and forms the clay to the desired shape and thickness. He may have to add more clay in the same way from time to time until the pot is completed. As the clay tends to dry out in the air and to become sticky, and finally brittle, the potter dips his hands in a dish of water conveniently placed on his worktable. He thus keeps the material at the proper consistency for modeling. If he should make a mistake or accidentally crack or bend or mar the half-finished piece of work, he crushes the whole together in his hands, mixes it with a little water, and starts over from the beginning.

Holy Scripture refers to the potter and his clay to illustrate the relation of God to His people. "Then I went down to the potter's house, and there he was, making something at the wheel. And the vessel that he made of clay was marred in the hand of the potter; so he made it again into another vessel, as it seemed good to the potter to make. Then the word of the LORD came to me, saying: 'O house of Israel, can I not do with you as this potter?' says the LORD. 'Look, as the clay is in the potter's hand, so are you in My hand, O house of Israel!'" (Jeremiah 18:3–6).

Isaiah confessed: "But now, O LORD, You are our Father; we are the clay, and You our potter; and all we are the work of Your hand" (Isaiah 64:8). Paul uses the same picture when he says, "But indeed, O man, who are you to reply against God? Will the thing formed say to him who formed it, 'Why have you made me like this?' Does not the potter have power over the clay, from the same lump to make one vessel for honor and another for dishonor?" (Romans 9:20–21).

When finished with the piece of pottery, the craftsman carefully sets it on a shelf, out of the wind and the sun. There it can dry uniformly and not too rapidly for several days—so that it will not crack nor check. The potter needed a practiced eye, steady hands, and just the right pressure of the fingers to do a good job. He needed the coordination of an artist. This trade tended to be passed down in the families.

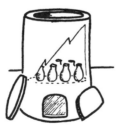

Small pottery kiln

Firing the pottery. After he has accumulated quite a number of finished pieces, the potter is ready to bake, or *fire,* them in a kiln of brick or stone—built for that purpose. Here

116

the dull pinkish-gray pieces are set up carefully in circular rows, tier above tier, so that the heat can get at them uniformly on all sides. Then the potter makes a small fire in the oven, gradually adding fuel until it becomes very hot. The fuelmay be chaff, brush wood, thorns, or anything else he can find. Each piece of new pottery becomes fused or melted together, with a texture similar to that of inexpensive red flowerpots. Then gradually the fire is permitted to die down and go out, and the kiln cools off gradually for a day or more. When it has completely cooled, the potter carefully removes the contents. This once-fired pottery is completely satisfactory for many purposes. It may be used for storing grain, raisins, dates, figs, and other foodstuffs.

Not all pottery can stand the fire. Some pieces crack because they do not fire uniformly. Others become too hot and melt, so that the neck or handle may sag. These will be thrown away on the pile outside or sold cheaply. Even a "precious vessel" cannot be put together again; they are as useless as the cheapest fragments: "You shall fall like a precious vessel" (Jeremiah 25:34). "I am forgotten like a dead man, out of mind; I am like a broken vessel" (Psalm 31:12). Even the potsherds (fragments) are not useless; they are broken into fine bits and used as we use sand in plaster and mortar.

pottery shapes

The glazing process; fine pottery. Containers for water and particularly for the storage of precious liquids must go through another process, called glazing. A very thin, creamy solution of an especially fine clay containing silica, or glass, is prepared. The pottery is either dipped into it or flushed or painted with it. This process deposits a thin but tough coating of clay. When baked in a very hot fire, this melts and runs to a glossy-smooth finish. By using colored pigment in the clay mixture, any desired color may be obtained in the glazing. A pattern may also be painted over the flush coat before the firing process. This design, too, will be fused into the glazed finish.

Finely formed and delicately worked earthenware has always been the pride of the potter. Drawings and photographs give us a general idea of the art. However, to appreciate the painstaking effort, the clever handiwork, and the artistic touch of the ancient potter, one must examine the collections in a museum and then try to make it. Pottery dumps often lead archaeologists to correct sites for their operations. Also the types and artistry of the potsherds in the fill help date the civilization.

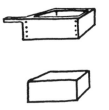

Brick mold and brick

Brick making. Though related to the work of the potter and often performed by him, the art of making bricks was not nearly as complicated as that of making pottery. Damp clay prepared in the potter's field was tightly packed into molds the size of the brick desired. Topless and bottomless, the mold was made of four thin wooden boards. A handle projected from one or two of them. As the clay dried, it shrank slightly, and the form could be removed easily. The bricks were then permitted to dry in the sun. Next, the workman piled them up in tiers, allowing a little air space between each two bricks. A fire built within the hollow brick structure cured them in the same way as the pottery described above.

Glazed bricks were produced by coating the once-fired brick on one side or all around with fine clay glazing material. It was then burned in a very intense heat. Colored glaze resulted from pigment added to the finish before the second baking. In the common bricks, particularly those that were merely baked in the sun, chopped straw was often used as bonding material to make the bricks more durable (Exodus 5:7).

The Metalworker

Varieties and sources of metals used. Though God had promised His people "a land whose stones are iron and out of whose hills you can dig copper" (Deuteronomy 8:9), Israel did not conquer and hold much of the mining country. She was always poor in the production of metal. Except when her boundaries were extended far to the north, or when her kings were strong enough to demand quantities of metal as tribute during the reigns of David and Solomon, she had to import most of her metal from other countries. Her wheat, olive oil, and wine were traded to Tarshish in Spain in return for silver, iron, tin, and lead (Ezekiel 27:12). Metal played a significant part in ancient Palestinian life. The chief metals used were iron, copper, lead, zinc, tin, silver, and gold.

Miner's tools: pick-ax, shovel, mallet, bar, and chisel

Workable quantities of iron in various compounds occur in the mountains of Syria. Palestine proper has no large iron deposits. Copper, sometimes found in an almost pure state in the mines, is the easiest of the materials to work. Though very tough, it is soft. Copper is often combined with tin to form bronze or combined with zinc to form brass. Both these alloys are much harder than the copper itself, and nearly as tough. Lead is found in considerable deposits in the Peninsula of Sinai. Gold was obtained from Sheba and Ophir (1 Kings 10:2; 22:48).

The smelting process. The ancient mining country to the north was also the heavily forested mountain region. Here the miner dug the metal ore out of the hills with pickax, crowbar, and shovel. The ore was taken in carts or on the backs of donkeys to the smelter—a stone or firebrick furnace arranged so that the ore could be mixed with charcoal. The entire contents of the furnace were then brought to a white heat. At this stage the metal ran out from the rock and charcoal, and congealed in forms provided for that purpose. Thus gold or silver, tried in the fire, lost the baser materials, the rock, the dross, and dust, with which it had been mixed, and became fine gold or fine silver (Proverbs 25:4; Malachi 3:3).

Clay molds for metal

Metal casting. The metalworker had a well-equipped metalworker's shop. It contained a small smelter in which the rough chunks of iron or copper or bits of scrap metal could be melted down in a charcoal flame. This flame was brought to a white heat by a blast of air from a bellows made of undressed skins of goat, usually worked by the foot (Jeremiah 6:29).

An Egyptian monument shows such a bellows arrangement. It consisted of two accordionlike air chambers made of wood and goatskin leather. A man operated them with his feet. He stood on them, alternately stretching and compressing the bellows by raising and lowering his feet in a tramping motion. An arrangement of simple valves prevented the air from flowing back into the bellows at each upward stroke. The air blasted instead through a pipe in the bottom of the smelter pit. The metal became red-hot, and then white-hot. Finally it began to run like syrup. The workman caught it in a fire-clay ladle and poured it into molds of the same material. There it hardened in the desired shape.

Forge, bellows, and
crucibles

Metalworker's tools:
hammers, chisel, and
tongs

Metal forging. Suppose that the object just cast in one of the molds is an iron axhead. It is not yet in its finished form, but rough and somewhat blunt. The metalworker lights up his forge, a smaller furnace similar to the smelter. When the charcoal is hot, he places the newly cast axhead into the hottest coals until it glows with a white heat. Then he grips it with a pair of iron tongs and takes it quickly to the anvil, a heavy block of iron or of hard stone. With a hammer he now beats it into the exact shape he wants. At the same time he sharpens the cutting edge by hammering it out to a knifelike thinness. He may have to reheat it several times during the process in order to make a good job. When he is finished, he allows it to cool or tempers it by dropping it into a pot of cold water. Finally, he sharpens the edge by rubbing it on a hard stone and fits a wooden handle into the head. In the same way blacksmiths also made plowshares, mattocks, forks, and goads.

Thus each individual bronze or iron tool, sword, or spear- head was made by hand from the time of Tubalcain (Genesis 4:22), all through Bible times, and almost to our own day. During the last years of the period of the Judges, Israel was so thoroughly subjugated by her enemies that no blacksmith shop was permitted to operate, not even to repair and sharpen agricultural implements. The people had to be satisfied to sharpen their implements with files (1 Samuel 13:9–21).

Making a bowl out of a copper sheet

Sheet metalworking. The copper in Palestine was used primarily in the form of thin sheets. These were worked up into various utensils called "articles of bronze" in the Old Testament (Exodus 27:3; 2 Samuel 8:10; 2 Chronicles 4:16). Cast into sheets as thin as possible, the metal was beaten or cast to uniform thickness. It was then cut into the desired shape for hammering.

Suppose that a washbasin-shaped copper bowl is to be made. The workman cuts out a circle of sheet copper with a chisel, holds it by the outer rim between his thumb and forefinger, and lets the center of it rest on his anvil or on a piece of very hard wood or lead. He lightly and rapidly taps it with a round-headed hammer. As he gradually rotates it, the hammer taps move in a gradually widening spiral toward the outer rim. He repeats this process over and over. Soon the sheet becomes slightly concave, and then more and more so, until the metal has been stretched to the required depth and shape. He now hammers a rim around the edge, makes the required handles out of the same metal, and rivets them in place. Then he polishes the finished product with sand or rock dust until it glistens in the light.

Cups and bowls, pitchers and plates, ladles and spoons were hammered out of sheet metal. Knives, saws, sickles, and other tools and implements were also products of the metalworker's shop. Ancient Damascus, capital of Syria, developed metalworking to a high degree of perfection, as did the Babylonians, Egyptians, and the Israelites themselves.

The gold- and silversmith. In a very refined way the processes described above were also used in the production of utensils and jewelry of the precious metals, gold and silver. The smelters, hammers, tongs, refining pots, and chisels or engraving tools and anvils were smaller. Proverbs 17:3, Ezekiel 22:18, and Zechariah 13:9 refer to the firing pot and furnace. The metals themselves were easier to work without heating. Thus the gold- or silversmith was able to produce work of the finest quality out of these precious metals (Isaiah 40:19; 41:7; Acts 19:24). They also understood the methods of smoothing or polishing (1 Kings 7:45), soldering (Isaiah 41:7), hammering out into plates (Numbers 16:38–39), gilding (overlaying with thin gold leaf), and cutting gold thread for embroidery (Exodus 28:6, 15). Silver tarnishes easily and eventually disintegrates through oxidation, but gold retains its brilliance much longer. The craftsmen who created the fine work of gold, silver, and brass in the temple devoted their best artistic efforts to the service of God (1 Kings 7:13–51).

The Tanner and Leather Worker; Other Trades

Location and equipment of tanneries. It is not by accident that the house of Simon, the tanner with whom Peter lodged in Joppa, was by the seaside (Acts 10:6). There were at least three reasons for this: the need for a plentiful supply of water, the need for a place to drain off used chemical refuse, and the social pressure that forced such an offensive trade away from the better residential neighborhoods to the already smelly waterfront. The tanner needed a house or a shop for the storage of his hides as well as for the large vats and tanks in which he cured the leather. He did this along the dock.

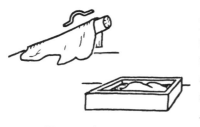

Tanner's log, scraper, and vat

Curing and tanning the hides. As the hides came from the slaughterer, they still had the hair of the animal on one side and a layer of fatty tissue and dried blood on the other. All loose matter was scraped off by laying the hide over a log set in the sandy beach or in the floor of the shop at an angle of about 30 degrees. In this scraping process the craftsman used a curved instrument, somewhat like a modern carpenter's drawknife, with which he scraped the hide on the flesh side. Next he soaked the hide in a vat containing a solution of lime or lye. This loosened the hair and the fatty matter still remaining. Putting it back on his log once more, he scraped it again until it was clean and soft. After carefully rinsing it in clean water, he immersed it in a tanning solution. We do not know the exact formula of the ancient tanning compounds. No doubt they were made of the bark of certain types of oak trees that are still used to cure the rawhide into leather. If soft leather was desired, the worker rubbed the skin with animal oil, similar to neat's-foot oil, and kneaded and scraped it until it was thoroughly dry. The leather could be dyed any color or given any desired finish.

(The same dyes and similar processes have been described in this chapter under "Dyeing and Bleaching.")

Water bottles. In modern Palestine hides that are to be used as water bottles were filled (stuffed) with oak chips. They were then filled with a strong solution of oak bark, which is largely tannic acid. The hair is fixed so that it will not drop out. After four months bottles are emptied out and used as containers to haul water. They are shipped to Syria, Egypt, and Mesopotamia, as they may have been in ancient times. "Bottles" in the Old Testament indicate that the process was known and used extensively then. The trade of tanner is mentioned only in Acts 9:43, 10:6, and 10:32. Male water carriers use such water skins; women use earthen jars.

Leather-working tools and leather goods. The tanner himself might be a leather worker, or he might sell his product to one who made a specialty of this highly developed craft. The leather worker needed a low bench, similar to one used by cobblers during the early 20th century. He had various types and sizes of awls—sharp nail-like pieces of metal held in a wooden handle. He used knives of several shapes to cut his leather, and needles and waxed linen thread to sew it up into the various articles. He also had tools to press patterns into the leather, like those that leather craftsmen use today. He worked up heavy cowhide into soles of sandals, various parts of soldier's armor, aprons for workmen, belts, etc. He used the finer types of leather for shoes and purses for the wealthy (Ezekiel 16:10). Fine ram skins dyed red, as well as badger (NIV—sea cow) skins, were used extensively in the construction of the Tabernacle (Exodus 25:5).

Leather worker's tools: awls, needles, knives, and bench

Tent making. The apostle Paul learned tent making in his youth and followed it at various times during his missionary career (Acts 18:3). It was a very lucrative trade. Tent cloth made from the goats' hair of Cilicia was of special high quality. It was used as sails, waterproof covering for the cargo being carried by camels, and also for tents. Except for military ships, ships in the first century depended on wind blowing against the sails for movement.

In the nomadic East, tents of all kinds found a ready market. Because of the extreme glare of the sun, the owners fitted their houses with awnings of all kinds. These kept the interior in semidarkness and provided porch space in the street. Tents of all shapes described in chapter 5 were the product of the tent maker.

Tent makers made the fabric for their best tents of goat's hair (Exodus 25:4). Others were made of cotton or of coarser fibers. For tools they used knives, shears, awls, and needle and thread—very similar to the tools of the leather workers.

Tools of the stonecutter: hammer, mallet, chisel, and saw

Stonecutting. Palestine was richly blessed with good limestone. The stonecutter's art flourished, particularly in the time of David and Solomon and up to the captivity, and again at the time of the Herods, when great building projects sprang up.

The ancient stonecutter took great blocks of stone from the quarries. He used pickaxes and crowbars, supplemented by chisels, mallets, saws, and drills, similar to those used by the carpenter. He also used a set of hammers with different types of edges—flat for cracking stones, sharp for splitting, toothed for dressing. Using a saw, newly exposed limestone can be cut almost as easily as ice. A drill point of iron or flint readily ground its way into the rock.

In order to split off a large slab of rock, the worker might drill a row of holes to a depth of about six inches. He then inserted a wedge of wood into each hole and tapped each wedge lightly with a hammer, again and again in rotation all along the row, until the desired stone block split off clean. Sometimes he forced pegs tightly into the holes and kept them soaked with water until the expansion of the water-soaked wood split off the rock. Using an iron chisel and mallet, or a stonecutter's hammer, he then dressed the stone down to the desired shape and smoothness.

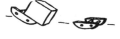

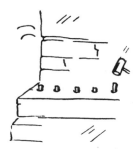

Method of splitting rock

Stone rockers and sled
on rollers

The stonecutter made sills and lintels ("headers") for doors and windows, paving blocks for fine buildings, carved stones to be used in doorway arches or as the heads of pillars and columns, great cylindrical sections of columns for the support of porches or colonnades, and stone benches for formal gardens and courtyards. He also made mills, mortars, and other stone implements and utensils.

The large blocks of stone were laboriously moved on low heavy-wheeled carts or on rollers. These jobs required the power of many men and animals.

The gem cutter. The ancient gem cutter was perhaps both a goldsmith and a jeweler. He became adept in cutting, grinding, and polishing precious and semiprecious stones of all kinds for bracelets, necklaces, strings of beads, pendants, and rings. He also made little flasks and boxes for cosmetics and ointments. His hammers, chisels, files, and drills were similar to those of the stonecutter, but much smaller and more carefully made.

The day laborer. Day laborers were ready to help out the home tradesman in his shop, when needed, or to furnish the bulk of the common labor for the larger operator or contractor. They were too poor or lacking the aptitude, experience, or initiative to have an independent trade of their own. Day laborers, especially in the larger towns and cities, came to the marketplace or gates early in the morning to look for a job for the day.

Agricultural laborers—with their shovels or mattocks or pruning hooks, depending on the seasons—waited, hopeful that some vineyard owner or farmer would hire them for the usual pay for one who worked by the day (Matthew 20:1–16). Carpenter helpers, plaster mixers, stone carriers, or woodcutters waited until the hiring for the day had been finished. If not hired, they dejectedly walked home or looked for a job in another part of town.

These people needed their pay each day. They and their families were often on the brink of starvation. Therefore God had specified in Deuteronomy 24:14–15 "You shall not oppress a hired servant who is poor and needy … . Each day you shall give him his wages, and not let the sun go down on it, for he is poor and has set his heart on it."

Review Questions and Exercises

1. How was the weaving of mats and baskets especially suited for home industry? Describe the process.
2. Describe the common tools used by the village carpenter. What were the main products he made?
3. Why was the potter's trade so important for life in Palestine? Describe the process a potter used to make a water container.
4. Why was leather so important for life in Palestine? List common articles made of leather.

5. From what materials was a tent normally made? In his earlier life, what kind of material did the apostle Paul use to make tent cloth? For what was this tent cloth used besides tentmaking? Why?

Additional Activities

1. Try to weave a sample mat or piece of cloth.
2. Expand the picture of God as the Potter and His people as clay in His hands. Apply the Scripture references of Isaiah 64:8 and Jeremiah 18:3–6 to the life of a Sunday school teacher as modeled by God. What instrument does He use in this process?
3. Try to make a small pot from clay. You may bake it in the sun or in an oven at home.

Chapter 7

The Arts and Sciences; Travel, Trade, and Commerce

Each craft and trade discussed in chapter 6 involves a certain amount of artistry. The carpenter was a tradesman; yet when he worked at fine carpentry or wood carving or inlay work of wood and ivory, he became an artist. The stonecutter engaged in a trade; yet when he did intricate stone carving, and particularly when he worked on precious stones, his craft became an art. A metalworker became an artist as he did the finer work in gold and silver. So, too, did the potter as he applied the finest material and workmanship to the development of his art.

The Arts

Sculpture. The ancient Egyptians, Babylonians, Phoenicians, Syrians, Persians, Greeks, and Romans devoted much of their art to the making of images, shrines, models of temples, or of other articles connected with idolatrous worship. Demetrius and his fellow silversmiths made their craft into a prosperous art (Acts 19:24–28). Knowing human failings and sinfulness, the Lord gave this prohibition in the First Commandment: "You shall not make for yourself any carved image, or any likeness of anything that is in heaven above, or that is in the earth beneath, or that is in the water under the earth; you shall not bow down to them nor serve them. For I, the LORD your God, am a jealous God" (Exodus 20:4–5; see Deuteronomy 4:16–19; 27:19).

God here was not prohibiting all artistic designs and figures. He Himself included artistic designs and figures of flowers, fruits, palms, oxen, and even of cherubim in the specifications He provided for the tabernacle and the temple. What God meant in Exodus 20:3–4 was this: "You shall not make any carved images nor any likeness of anything on the earth in order to bow down to them or to worship them." This principle permitted the bronze oxen to hold up the bronze basin in the temple.

Once, however, Israel made golden calves *for worship,* repeating what Israel had done in Moses' absence on Mount Sinai in the wilderness (Exodus 32:1–2). They worshiped Jeroboam's calves at Bethel and Dan (1 Kings 12:26–33). God's prophet plainly warned against the abuse and announced a curse upon Jeroboam (1 Kings 13:1–2). Later, at Ahab's time, Israel fell even deeper into gross worship of the Baal images (1 Kings 16:30–33; 18:17–46). So also did Judah in later years, disregarding the warnings of Isaiah, Jeremiah, and the other prophets (Isaiah 44:9–10; Jeremiah 10:3–4). Finally God took away His people into bondage (2 Chronicles 36:17–21).

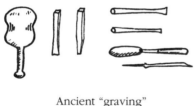

Ancient "graving" tools

In heathen Babylon, amid idolatrous worshipers, the people of Israel turned away from the tendency to become idolaters themselves. After they returned to Palestine, under Ezra and Nehemiah, we find no further evidence of idol worship. Instead, the rabbis prohibited everything that might even suggest idolatry. No images of animals or angels appeared in the new temple or in the local synagogs. Josephus, the Jewish historian, says that even in the homes of the wealthy such decoration was forbidden (Josephus, *Antiquities,* 17, 6, 2; Josephus, *Wars,* 2, 10, 4). This spirit prompted the defeated Jews not to allow their Roman conquerors to march into Jerusalem carrying the emperor's image on their standards (*Antiquities,* 18, 3, 1; *Wars,* 2, 9, 2).

The pressure of this puritanic trend discouraged sculpturing almost to the point of extinction. Religious leaders feared that artistic productions might become a snare to the people and should therefore be omitted.

A similar example existed in American history. The bare "meeting houses" of the American Puritans reflected the Calvinistic view that the use of everything that Roman Catholics had devoted to idolatrous purposes (such as crosses, crucifixes, and statues) might tempt the people to commit idolatry.

Egyptian paintbrushes of fiber

Painting. Painting developed to a remarkable level in Egypt. Here the Hebrews must have learned, or at least have observed, its methods and techniques. Back in Palestine, however, the people of Israel did not develop the art, as far as we know. Thus, we know exactly what many ancient Pharaohs looked like, along with hundreds of other heathen dignitaries of Old Testament times, but we have no pictures or statues of Moses, David, Solomon, Isaiah, or Daniel. While we have exact knowledge of the appearance of Julius Caesar, Augustus, Tiberius, and Nero, we do not know what Matthew, Luke, Paul, or Jesus Himself may have looked like.

Writing and writing materials. Some method of recording thought is necessary for the development of ideas in the sciences. This is true to the extent that people who were not able to write have never advanced very far culturally.

Job (probably a contemporary of Abraham, forefather of the Israelites) wished that his words might be written in a book (Job 19:23). At the time of Abraham the Babylonians had already recorded their complete set of laws and many other literary works. By the time of the exodus the art of composition was highly developed. Moses, who had been educated by the Egyptians, could write a set of five books that tell the history of his people and a record of God's directions for their faith and lives. While these books are *God's* Word, they are also the finest product of *human* writing in the literature of the period. At the time of the exodus writing must have been common, at least among the professional classes, the judges and the priests (Exodus 17:14; Deuteronomy 24:1ff; Numbers 5:23).

Stylus and clay tablet—Mesopotamia

Parchment scroll
or "book"

The Babylonians wrote their literary works, letters, bills, and receipts on small tablets of clay. They pressed a chisel-like stylus into soft clay to make the wedge-shaped characters. Then they allowed the clay to dry or even baked it to make it durable. If the message was particularly important, they covered it with another thin coating of clay, both to keep its contents secret and to protect it from rough handling. Important proclamations and other documents were chiseled into the solid rock, or on monuments or on stone slabs, as were the Ten Commandments that God gave to Moses (Exodus 31:18; 32:15–16).

The Israelites ordinarily wrote their important documents upon parchment, the skin of goats or sheep. Carefully scraped until it was thin and clean and almost transparent, it was then smoothed out until it became a fine-textured writing surface. The Hebrews wrote in columns from right to left. When he had finished his writing, the scribe rolled up his parchment strip into a scroll (Psalm 40:7; Jeremiah 36:23).

The Israelites may also have used papyrus, as did the Egyptians. Egyptians made papyrus of the inner layers of the papyrus stalk. After unrolling the layers from a length of the stalk, they laid them flat, side by side on a smooth wet surface.

Then they laid another thickness on top of them at right angles and pressed the two layers together. When dry, they became one sheet of very strong paper.

Papyrus reed and
method of making paper

Scribe's stylus
and inkhorn

Scribes. A scribe wrote letters for others—particularly legal papers, business contracts, and other important documents—especially when someone needed two or more copies. He affixed his seal to testify to the signatures or seals of the party or parties. The scribe commonly carried papers or parchment, his stylus, and a horn of ink at his girdle (Ezekiel 9:2). The writer used a stylus of reed or of wood, which he dipped in black ink (Jeremiah 36:18; 2 John 12). Many scribes were constantly employed to copy the Old Testament Scriptures and other religious writings. The New Testament usually groups them with the Pharisees, as "scribes and Pharisees." *Scribes* in the New Testament refers especially to those who were deeply involved in studying the Old Testament Scriptures and other religious writings of that time.

Literature. The Bible is God's inspired Word. Yet each of the Hebrew writers has left the stamp of his own style on his writings. The Old Testament consists of several types of literature. Historical books, with the covenant guidelines, prophecies, and doctrines woven into them, give us a connected story of God's people. They also provide a clear picture of their virtues, their sins, their repentance, and their hope of salvation. Poetic books, including Job, the Psalms, Proverbs, and

Ecclesiastes, teach us God's will and help us worship Him. The prophetic books point to the great events of the future and, above all, to the coming of the Savior. All these books together form a complete literature. Nothing like it appears elsewhere in world history.

During and after the exile the people of Israel produced many other religious books modeled after the Scriptures themselves. Some of these form the Old Testament Apocrypha. These were often printed in the older Bibles along with the canonical books. The Roman Catholic Church regards them as part of the Holy Scriptures. We have the titles or very brief descriptions or excerpts of many other books. In the centuries just before the coming of Jesus the Jews of the Dispersion produced an abundance of religious literature. Instead of Hebrew, these were written in everyday Aramaic or, like the New Testament books, in Greek, the literary language of the day. For example, the Dead Sea Scrolls were written in Hebrew and Aramaic.

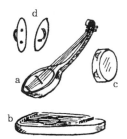

Musical instruments: (a) kinnor, (b) instrument of 10 strings, (c) tambourine, (d) cymbals

Music and musical instruments. We know very little about ancient music, not even the intervals of the scale employed. No doubt it would sound strange and weird to us today. The various instruments played only the melody, in contrast to the harmonies of our modern orchestration.

The invention of musical instruments goes back to Jubal, a descendant of Cain, who was "the father of all those who play the harp and flute" (Genesis 4:21). These two types (string and wind instruments), along with the percussion devices, include all the musical instruments mentioned in the Bible.

A stringed instrument, the kinnor, or harp (1 Samuel 16:23), probably was similar to a guitar. It was played with the fingers (1 Samuel 18:10) or with a wooden or bone plectrum. This instrument had gut strings and a stretched-skin sounding board. Musicians could even play it walking (1 Samuel 10:5; 2 Samuel 6:5). The "instrument of ten strings" (Psalm 33:2) consisted of a shallow oblong box. The strings were metal wires stretched across the wooden sounding board. Great varieties of harps, guitars, and lyres appear on the Egyptian monuments. Undoubtedly many of these were also used in Palestine, though it is difficult to make a positive identification in any Scripture references.

The timbrel, or tambourine, was light wooden hoop with rawhide stretched tightly across its surface, and disks of metal set into slits in the wooden rim. Women usually used this very popular percussion instrument. They shook it rhythmically with one hand and tapped the rawhide surface with the fingers of the other hand as they kept time for their ceremonial dancing (Judges 11:34—Jephtha's daughter). Cymbals, disks of brass (1 Chronicles 15:19) that were clashed together, were used in the temple service (1 Chronicles 25:1, 6). The sistrum was a large metal ring from which hung smaller rings and bars of metal (2 Samuel 6:5).

Wind instruments: horn and trumpet of brass, ram's horn and cow-horn trumpets, flute and double flute

The pipe, or flute, made of reed, was a *wind instrument.* A favorite instrument of country folk, it provided music for weddings or for funerals or for whiling away the time of the lonely shepherds (Matthew 9:23; Revelation 18:22; Isaiah 5:12). As far as we know, it was not used in public worship. The cornet, or the trumpet, had a brilliant, penetrating tone. It developed from the curved horn of an animal, but later was made of silver. Like our church bells, it called people to worship. Instead of being bent into an elongated coil, like trumpets today, it was left in one long straight tube with a

135

flared-out end. The horn, or trombone, had a lower pitch but a very penetrating tone. It was also used at religious services. The sackbut was a stringed instrument in triangular form with a shrill penetrating sound.

Rejoicing over their deliverance from Pharaoh's host, Miriam and the other women went out "with timbrels and with dances," chanting the praises of God for His mercy to them (Exodus 15:20). This was also done at the observance of the major festivals of rejoicing (1 Kings 1:40). Solemn chanting marked the periods of national or family mourning (Jeremiah 9:17–18; 2 Chronicles 35:25; Matthew 9:23).

Girls and women danced among themselves for social pastime (Jeremiah 31:4). The children of the street were as quick to imitate their elders in dancing as in mourning (Luke 7:32; Job 21:11). Occasionally, too, we hear of men dancing under the stress of great emotion, as when David and his men danced before the Ark of the Lord (2 Samuel 6:5; 2 Samuel 6:14).

Ancient dancing consisted of rhythmic steps in circular movements, accompanied by the tapping of tambourines or the rhythm of other percussion instruments. We find no trace of dancing between the sexes. Nor do we find any sign that female dancers indulged in the shameless motions and exposure that were common among the Greeks and Romans of New Testament times. For instance, when Herodia's daughter, Salome, danced before Herod (Matthew 14:6), she was probably carrying out a Roman custom that fit in very well with the rest of the wantonness and debauchery of a typical Roman feast.

The Sciences

Consciousness of nature. The Old Testament, particularly the psalms of David and the works of Solomon, reveals a consciousness of nature. David, the shepherd boy, alone in the hills with his sheep, developed a close kinship with God's lowliest creatures. Jesus showed a similar kinship by His interest in the lilies of the field, the fowl of the air (Matthew

6:26–28), and the two sparrows sold for a copper coin (Matthew 10:29). Solomon "spoke of trees, from the cedar tree of Lebanon even to the hyssop that springs out of the wall; he spoke also of animals, of birds, of creeping things, and of fish" (1 Kings 4:33). Many of Solomon's writings must not have come down to us. The book of Job, too, shows a broad knowledge of nature.

However, the Bible is not a textbook of botany or zoology; it merely mentions these things in passing. The later rabbinical literature shows a considerable interest in nature. They combined a strange mixture of speculation and superstition with scientific knowledge, but the Israelites did not practice science as we know it today.

Medicine and healing. Since the fall the human race has been subject to illness, which is the result of sin and a foretaste of death. The Bible contains many references to sickness and to healing; yet we cannot tell how much the ancient Israelites knew about disease. No doubt they became acquainted with the medical practices of Egypt and in New Testament times with those of the Greeks and Romans. Luke was the beloved physician of Paul (Colossians 4:14) and remained with him when Paul needed him most (2 Timothy 4:11).

We have very little information concerning the extent to which internal medicine was prescribed. At least the upper classes had the services of physicians in Old Testament times (2 Chronicles 16:12). Luke tells of the unfortunate woman with an issue of blood "who had spent all her livelihood on physicians and could not be healed by any" (Luke 8:43). Mark puts it much more bluntly: she "had suffered many things from many physicians. She had spent all that she had and was no better, but rather grew worse" (Mark 5:25–26).

No doubt the common people had to rely on their own home remedies passed down from generation to generation. In chapter 3 we noted the use of dried fruits, olive oil, and the roughage in whole wheat flour and other foods. This reduced the need for physics and purgatives that have become so common today.

External medication was used very extensively. Wounds and bruises were cleansed with water or with wine, anointed with olive oil, and then bandaged (Isaiah 1:6; Luke 10:34). Soothing ointments and salves were prepared from various herbs. The East Jordan country was famous for the balm of Gilead, made of the sap of a tree (Jeremiah 8:22; 46:11). Lumps of boiled figs served as poultices for boils (2 Kings 20:7).

Warm medicinal springs still exist in the Dead Sea area. According to Josephus, Herod went there for relief from his ailment (*Antiquities,* 16, 6,5; *Wars,* 1, 33, 5). Sufferers from rheumatism, arthritis, or the aches and pains of malaria would find welcome relief in such springs. The first symptoms of leprosy, the most dreaded of diseases, were carefully watched.

Recent studies and careful analysis by medical specialists, especially those who have dealt with Hansen's Disease (true leprosy), have shown that the Scriptures used the term leprosy for a variety of skin diseases. Anyone afflicted with these was removed from society (Leviticus 13). Jesus healed a number who suffered from these dreaded skin diseases (Mark 1:40–45; Luke 17:11–19). Palsy, or paralysis, was very common and considered incurable.

Acute eye infections, increased by the sun's glare and the dust in the trees, often led to blindness. The fine dust that blew off the great Arabian Desert also caused blindness. Most of the other diseases mentioned in the Bible have been identified, but we have little information about materials or methods used in their treatment. We do know, though, that they all yielded to the almighty power of Jesus, the Great Physician, as shown by His many miracles of healing.

Surgeons, using instruments remarkably like our own, attempted delicate operations of all kinds. These could not be very successful, however, without the knowledge of anesthetics and antiseptics. We have no information about how much the Jews practiced surgery.

Various kinds of charms and amulets are common in the Near Eastern countries today. Scripture, however, does not mention such faith-healing or magic devices.

Mathematics and physics. Moses learned some mathematics and astronomy from the Egyptians. We know that the Israelites in the wilderness could compute their weights and measures, as well as the dimensions and distances for the construction of the tabernacle. They also understood geometry, or "earth measurement," well enough to measure and allot land in Palestine at the time of Joshua. By New Testament times the physical sciences had advanced remarkably in the Greek world. No doubt Paul, Luke, and other well-educated men had a fair scientific knowledge. The Bible itself is silent on this point, however, as it is in so many others that are not vital to the central message of sin and grace.

Architecture. Painstaking detail was needed to construct the elaborate palace of David and of Solomon, and especially of the temple. This shows that the science of architecture had also advanced among the Israelites—although Hiram's Phoenician architects and craftsmen may have done much of this work. At the time of Jesus and Paul the architecture of Jerusalem and other large Jewish cities tended to be Greek or Roman rather than Jewish. The fine sense of proportion and balance and the solid construction of the ancient Greek public buildings have never been surpassed, except perhaps in our own generation. Outstanding examples of architecture in New Testament Jerusalem were the temple of Herod and the great palaces of the wealthy and of the priests. These people spared no expense to make those structures as outstanding as any of that day. Recent archaeological activities have helped us know about their size and beauty. This is true also of the great innovative engineering feat of the artificial harbor that Herod the Great had engineers build at Caesarea.

Astronomy. Like all the ancient nations of the Near East, the Hebrews were very conscious of the heavenly bodies. When God told Abraham to look to the heavens and count the stars (Genesis 15:5), they must have seemed so close to him that he could almost touch them. Stars still seem close in those regions today. The sun was extremely bright in the day time, and at night people thought the moon was dangerous (Psalm 121:6). The Hebrews recognized some constellations. Job mentions Arcturus, Orion, and Pleiades; and Amos speaks of "Pleiades and Orion" (Amos 5:8).

Time and the Calendar

Disregard of time; "the unhurried East." Still today many Western travelers are amazed by the seeming disregard of time in parts of the Near East. The rush and bustle of the Western world and especially of the United States may seem strange to people there. The ordinary units of time were the same among Bible peoples as they are now: the day, the week, the month, and the year.

The day; day and night. The Hebrew day began at sunset and ended at sunset of the next day (Genesis 1:5; Leviticus 23:32). Day and night averaged 12 hours each. They ranged from 10 to 14 hours in the various seasons. In ancient times it appears that the night was divided into three watches of four hours each (Judges 7:19). Later Jews adopted the plan common to the Roman Empire—four watches of three hours each. Jesus' illegal night trial before the Jewish Council took place during the third watch of the night, known as the cockcrow watch (Mark 14:53–72; John 18:15–18; 25–27). Wealthy people probably used a sundial (2 Kings 20:11; Isaiah 38:8). Very likely the water clock, used by neighboring peoples, also served to tell time in Palestine, at least from late Old Testament times on.

The week and month. A week contained six work days, followed by the Sabbath. Mosaic laws protected the sanctity of that day of rest.

Changing phases of the moon determined the Hebrew month. A sound of trumpets hailed the new moon as the beginning of another month. It appears that at first the Hebrews numbered their months and only in later times named them. Both names and numbers appear in various places in Scripture. Beginning in spring, the months ran as follows: Nisan, Iyar, Sivan, Tammuz, Ab, Elul, Tishri,

Marcheshvan, Chisleu, Tebeth, Shebat, Adar. The Hebrew calendar, which is a lunar calendar based on 12 lunar cycles, does not quite fit our solar calendar. It is adjusted to the solar calendar by adding a month according to certain cycles to keep festival days in synch. Thus, Nisan roughly corresponds with April, Iyar with May, and so forth.

The year. Nisan, or April, the opening of spring, began the year, according to the account in Exodus 12:2; 23:15. The whole Old Testament cycle of religious festivals is determined by this date.

The agricultural year, on the other hand, began in the fall (Exodus 23:16), as did the sabbatic years and the years of jubilee (Leviticus 25:9–10). There are really only two seasons in Palestine, summer and winter. Special seasonal periods occur at the time of the barley harvest in late spring, the wheat harvest in early summer, the harvest of grapes in early fall, and the time of sowing later in autumn. From the viewpoint of climate and moisture, the two seasons are the rainy and the dry seasons. The dry season begins early in May and ends in autumn. Dew provides the only moisture during this season. It is brought in daily in the evening by the cooling west and northwest breezes.

Travel and Transportation by Land and Sea

Travel in general. Since the time of Cain people tended to migrate to find new pastures, new agricultural land, new security, or new freedom (Genesis 4:16). The story of the patriarchs began with the command to Abraham, "Get out of your country, from your kindred and from your father's house, to a land that I will show you" (Genesis 12:1). A generation later Abraham's servant traveled to Mesopotamia to find a wife for Isaac. Isaac's son Jacob followed the same route to escape from his brother Esau. Traders bought Joseph from his brothers and took him along to Egypt, beginning a chain of events that led all of Israel to that country (Genesis 37:27; 46:6). For 40 years Israel traveled about in the wilderness of Sinai before each family finally received its allotment of land a generation later under Joshua. Trade and periodic festivals led to considerable travel on roads within the Holy Land itself. Jesus, like other young people, must have eagerly looked forward to the time when He would make one of these journeys for the first time (Luke 2:42).

Following lines of least resistance, Palestinian roads wound through valleys and gorges, along mountain ridges, and across fords in the river, as they had done for hundreds of years. People then usually walked as they traveled. Around 15 miles was a good day's journey. Travelers of today still cover about the same distances and stop at the same springs or wells of water. The average road was often poorly kept, dusty in summer, and often almost impassible in the rainy season.

In the remote regions, the roads were trails—or paths, as the Bible calls them. Often it was difficult to decide which path out of two or three was the one to take. "Show me Your ways, O Lord!" says the psalmist (Psalm 25:4). The main road from Jerusalem to Jericho, well traveled as it was, could be dangerous (Good Samaritan—Luke 10:34). The back roads would be more dangerous, especially in times of political unrest. There were no road maps. Travelers had to depend on their own sense of direction or the sometimes questionable guidance of a stranger. People did not travel often, except as a part of a caravan of friends. They calculated distance by the amount of time needed to cover the journey, not in miles.

Travel by foot. Bible people made very long journeys on foot. This meant that the travelers had to carry with them everything they needed on the way—staff, cloak for protection during the night, bag, food for the journey, and a jar or dried gourd filled with water (Genesis 21:14). The bag, made of leather, might contain dried fruit, nuts, parched wheat, and perhaps a little bread.

Thus equipped, whole companies traveled together on foot to attend the festivals of the Passover, the First Fruits (Pentecost), and the Feast of Booths (Harvest). Those coming from Galilee would normally walk down the east side of the Jordan Valley, which was much easier than walking through the hills and valleys of Samaria. By doing this they also avoided the enmity of the Samaritans. They probably camped out at night, and perhaps rested during the noon hours during the warmer season of the year. Perhaps some women and smaller children rode donkeys.

A khan

The inn, or khan, on the main roads. Inns were located at convenient stopping places. In its simplest form the inn might be an area surrounded by a stone wall, except for a strong door. Most contained a courtyard surrounded by rooms. The courtyard was open to the sky. Animals were kept there. Also, travelers camped there at times. Most inns were quite primitive.

A well-developed inn contained a courtyard into which a roof extended inward from the walls on all sides, forming a sort of shed all the way around the open court. This might be two stories high. The ground floor was rented to the travelers for their animals and baggage, and the people themselves lived in the upper story.

Travel by camel caravan. On the fringes of the wilderness and desert long-distance travelers formed camel trains. A group of merchants united for mutual companionship and protection. During the day the camels traveled single file, carrying their packs and at times their masters as well. Wagons, open or covered (Numbers 7:3), were used quite extensively in ancient times. The Egyptian Pharaoh sent wagons, probably drawn by chariot horses, to transport Joseph's family and the possessions to Egypt (Genesis 45:19 ff.).

In Palestine itself, as well as in the countries to the east oxen or cows normally served as draft animals (1 Samuel 6:7, 2 Samuel 6:6). Four-wheeled wagons appear in very early

143

Babylonian times. However, the people of Bible times, as well as those of the Near East of today, commonly used two-wheeled carts. Such a cart consisted of a wooden platform set on a heavy wooden axle, fitted with wooden wheels. The wheels were solid, sometimes made of three or four heavy planks of wood fastened together with two crosspieces, cut into circular shape, and held together by a tire of iron or rawhide. From the platform a tongue extended to which the yoke of the oxen was secured. (See chapter 2 on yokes.) Great trains of these wagons, each drawn by one or two teams of oxen, still would cross the plains of Mesopotamia in the early part of the 20th century.

Papyrus boat
Wooden boat

Boats, ferries, and rafts. In the Egyptian delta region the Israelites had seen various types of boats, from the small raftlike craft to the palatial yachts of the wealthy. On the Sea of Galilee small boats were used both for fishing and transportation (John 6:22). In many ways these resembled the simple wooden boat of today. They were built of boards overlapped on each other and caulked with fiber and pitch to make them watertight. A boat used about 2,400 years ago was recently found near the northwestern shore of the Sea of Galilee. Sometimes favorable winds made the use of sails possible (Luke 8:23), but ordinarily the boatmen had to depend on their oars. Rafts were made of inflated skins of animals covered by a platform of wood. Very buoyant, these were useful for ferrying heavy material across rivers.

Sailing and seagoing ships. The Old Testament and the book of Acts contain many references to ships and their various features. See Ezekiel 27 and Acts 20:13–16; 21:1–4, 7–8, and 27–28. Most ships in both the Old Testament and the New Testament areas had a mainsail (often with the top sails placed

Skin boat and raft

above it), the foresail on the prow (at the front of the ship), and two oarlike rudders that were used for steering. Apparently oars were used primarily on ships used in naval warfare. Cargo ships had a rounded hull and featured a raised prow and stern. In earlier eras the sails may have been made of linen from Egypt. Later, if not earlier, sails made from goats' hair (tent cloth) apparently were used universally. These were waterproof and very strong. Note that ancient people did not have compasses. Also, at the time of the New Testament they probably did not have nautical charts.

A naval vessel

The size of ships varied, depending on their purpose. The grain ship that was shipwrecked as recorded in Acts 27 must have been very large. Aside from its sizable grain cargo, it carried 276 people. A merchant ship that had sunk near Caesarea has recently been found. It was about 146 feet long. A grain ship also found recently was 180 feet long and 45 feet wide. It carried an estimated 1,200 tons of grain.

The safe sailing season began in the middle of March and ended in the middle of September. Sailing then became very dangerous, as Acts 27 records.

Sailing ceased completely about November 11. Under very favorable weather conditions, short distance trips resumed before the middle of March. Acts 28 records the safe voyage from Malta to the Puteoli during this period.

Palestine—sailing. The coastline of Palestine is rather

unfriendly. It had no good harbors. The harbor of Joppa had a line of rocks lying offshore. It was somewhat safe only when the sea winds were quiet. The Philistines developed some comparatively safe harbors at Ascalon and Ashdod, as recent excavations have shown. David developed trade relations with the Phoenicians, who had excellent harbors to the north. For centuries they were the merchant mariners on the Mediterranean. Because of their favorable trade relations with David and Solomon, the Phoenicians built a merchant marine for Solomon. It sailed down the Gulf of Aqaba to the Red Sea and beyond. In the last four centuries before Christ and throughout the New Testament times, great fleets of ships carried the goods of Egypt, Syria, Phoenicia, and Greece to the western Mediterranean as far as Rome, Sicily, and Spain. Paul suffered shipwreck on one of these ships. The story of the storm and wreck recorded by Luke in Acts 27:10–28:5 is considered the finest description of such a tragedy in all ancient literature.

Business Methods, Measures, Weights, Money
The spread of Jewish commerce in the Dispersion.
Several biblical people showed a strong business instinct. Jacob drove a hard bargain with his brother Esau (Genesis 25:29–34). His uncle Laban displayed a shrewdness that failed to draw a clear distinction between a sharp business deal and outright crookedness (Genesis 29:18–28; 30:27–43).

The Lord seems to have intended that His people earn their living under His divine blessing by working the rich soil He had allotted to them (Deuteronomy 16:15). With the surplus of the products of the pasture, the farmland, and the vineyard they were to trade with foreign nations for goods they themselves could not produce.

To better understand the history of God's covenant people—especially during the Old Testament—we need to remember that Palestine was the central span of the great international trade bridge. The most important trade routes of Palestine were the great Way of the Sea (*Via Maris*), which connected Egypt with Mesopotamia and the Orient, and the King's Highway, which ran from Damascus through the area east of the Jordan to the Gulf of Aqaba.

Much trade came down the Nile River from Southeast Central Africa. This trade, together with the products of Egypt—especially its grain—could be sent down the Nile to Alexandria. Much also went on the Way of the Sea across the northern area of the Sinai Peninsula to the coastal plain of Palestine. Then it went through the pass of Megiddo northeast to the shore of the Sea of Galilee at the Plain of Gennesaret. In the area of Bethsaida-Capernaum it turned north to cross the Jordan near Hazor, and then went on to Damascus. From there this trade route led into Northern Syria. One arm later turned southeast down the Euphrates River to the Persian Gulf and east to India and the Orient. Trade was carried by caravans of camels.

Grain, grapes, and olives were important for Palestine's export trade. The people also exported wool, linen, asphalt (from the region of the Dead Sea), and dates—especially from Jericho. They imported precious stones, ivory, incense, spices, costly cloth, and fine garments (Isaiah 60:6).

Local business—haggling over prices. World conditions affected the amount of export and import trade. Meanwhile, everybody at home did some buying. Many people sold primarily to the home market. Careful planning and finesse have always accompanied even small business deals in the Near East. Without haggling over prices, no bargain was satisfactory or complete, either to the buyer or to the seller. This is true yet in many cases today.

Fingerbreadth, palm, span, and cubit

Lineal measurement. No absolute and lasting standard of measurement, weight, or coinage existed in the ancient Near East. Therefore only approximate information can be given in the following paragraphs.

Since lineal measure was based on parts of the human body, it varied according to time

147

and country. The smallest unit was the fingerbreadth, somewhat less than an inch (Jeremiah 52:21). Four fingerbreadths equal a handbreadth, or palm (Exodus 37:12). Three palms equal one span, the distance from the tip of the thumb of an outstretched hand to the tip of the index finger (Exodus 28:16); some commentators suggest that a span is the distance between the end of the thumb and the little finger when outstretched. Two of these spans equal a cubit, which was the distance between the elbow and the tip of the longest finger. The many different cubits used in the Near East were about 18 inches and slightly longer. The Egyptian royal cubit measured 20.7 inches. Six cubits made one reed (Ezekiel 41:8), about 10 feet.

A man's step or pace, about 30 inches (2 Samuel 6:13), determined larger distances. "A little way" seems to have been slightly more than three miles (Genesis 48:7), about the distance one could conveniently walk in an hour. The "day's journey" was the distance traveled (usually by walking) during the day. Depending on the time of the year and the topography, a day's journey varied from around 15 to 20 miles. A Sabbath's day journey seems to have been around two-thirds of a mile (Acts 1:12).

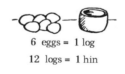

6 eggs = 1 log

12 logs = 1 hin

Liquid measure

Liquid and dry measure. The log was the smallest common unit for measuring liquids. A log was the amount of water six hen's eggs would displace, about a pint. Twelve logs made one hin, about six quarts, or one and one-half gallons. Six hins made one bath, about nine gallons. The water jars mentioned in John 2:6 held about 18 to 27 gallons. A homer, or cor, equaled 10 baths, or about 90 gallons.

A cab, a little less than two quarts, was the smallest unit of dry measure. Six cabs made one seah, not quite 10 quarts.

Three seahs made one ephah, about a bushel. Ten ephahs made one homer, the largest common unit, about 10 bushels. The Roman *modius* (translated various ways) is about a peck, one quarter of a bushel. A container this size was very handy to have around the home.

Money. The study of coins in the ancient world is complicated. Coins had various sizes, shapes, and weight; the proportions of silver, gold, copper, and less expensive alloys varied; some people with little integrity made coins; and not all coins remained in use for long periods of time. Ancient coins did not have milled edges. Therefore one could not tell how much metal might have been worn or even filed off. We can only approximate values and modern equivalents, especially since the buying power of a coin also varied from time to time. Scripture does state, however, that a laborer was ordinarily paid a denarius for a day's work (Matthew 20:2).

Lumps of silver served as money in earliest time. These lumps had to be weighed each time they were used, since small chunks could easily be chipped off. As early as the time of Sarah's death, marked silver was in use. Abraham paid for the Cave of Machpelah as a family burial place in "shekels of silver, currency of the merchants" (Genesis 23:16). That is, he paid with silver pieces, each weighing a shekel and so marked. The bekah was a half shekel. The gerah was one-twentieth of a shekel.

In New Testament times the lepton was the smallest copper coin (Mark 12:42; Luke 12:6). The silver stater, which Peter found in the mouth of the fish, was worth four denarii. With it he paid the temple tax for Jesus and for himself (Matthew 17:27). The New Testament talent was worth about 6,000 denarii. Since the value of these coins changed from one period to another, it is difficult to estimate their value in today's currency.

During the centuries just before the birth of Christ, and in New Testament times, money from the Greek and Roman world, as well as that from the East, flowed freely in the markets of Palestine. The uncertain and changing values of the various coins provided opportunities for dishonesty. Shrewd money changers in the temple, grafting tax-collectors, and money-wise merchants became wealthy at the expense of the ignorant and the unfortunate.

Review Questions and Exercises

1. Why were God's people in Bible times not known for their paintings and sculpture?
2. What writing instruments did biblical people use?
3. Name some musical instruments that the Israelites used. What does Scripture tell about their use?
4. Which New testament writer was a doctor? How do we know this?
5. By what means of transportation did people travel from Galilee to Jerusalem? What route did they usually take? Why? Tell about their overnight lodging.
6. How did the winds on the Mediterranean affect sailing? Which were the favorable winds for sea travel? Why are Acts 20, 21, and 27–28 so important for those wanting to learn about sailing during biblical times?

Additional Activities

1. Find several nature psalms. What do you learn about life in Palestine from them?
2. On a Bible map trace the sea journey of Paul and his companions (Acts 21:13–16; 21:1–9). About how far did they travel each day?
3. Describe the money used in the New Testament era. Why was the denarius so important at that time?

Chapter 8

Social Customs
and Family Life

Each nation and age in history has its distinctive social customs. Customs in the Near East did not change much from century to century. Until recent years rural and village life in Palestine mirrored many of the habits and practices from biblical times.

Care of the Body; Dress and Adornment

Washing, bathing, and anointing. The law of Moses commanded bathing both for physical cleanliness and as a religious ceremony. Already at the time of Jacob pure bodies symbolized purity from sin (Genesis 35:2). Special purifications were ordered on special occasions throughout Israel's history (Joshua 3:5). Even Pilate washed his hands before the Jews to claim innocence of the crime of killing Jesus (Matthew 27:24). Years earlier David spoke of clean hands as a sign of innocence (Psalm 73:13).

People might bathe in a river, either for ordinary cleansing (Exodus 2:5) or to achieve Levitical purity. Well-equipped homes of the wealthy might have bathing facilities in the courtyard (2 Samuel 11:2) or in special rooms. A stone bathtub has been found in the remains of a Cretan civilization from the time of the exodus. This bathtub had running water and had drains for waste. At the time of Jesus the Greeks and Romans built extensive and luxurious public baths. To some degree we find similar arrangements in the larger Romanized cities of Palestine. Until very recent years people in these cities exhibited many biblical habits and practices.

After the bath people sometimes anointed the body with perfumed oil (Ruth 3:3). Palestine produced some perfumes, but many were imported from Sheba (1 Kings 10:10) and other countries. Nard, or "spikenard," with which Mary of Bethany anointed Jesus, was most costly. It was so strongly scented that "the house was filled with the fragrance of the oil" (John 12:3). It was worth about 300 denarii—a year's wages for a daily worker. The poor used ordinary olive oil instead of the perfumed variety. People anointed their head with olive oil, perfumed or otherwise, on festival days or as a sign of special favor (Psalm 23:4; Ecclesiastes 9:8).

People admired Absalom's long hair (2 Samuel 14:26), but some young people ridiculed Elisha for his baldness (2 Kings 2:23). Jews ordinarily cut their hair rather short with a razor (Ezekiel 44:20), but they did not shave their heads as the Egyptians did. The women always wore their hair long. Thus Mary of Bethany could wipe Jesus' feet with her hair after she had anointed them with the precious ointment (John 12:1–3; 11:2). At the time of the early church people viewed short hair worn by women as a sign of doubtful morals, while "if a woman has long hair, it is a glory to her, for her hair is given to her for a covering" (1 Corinthians 11:15). Women usually braided their hair or put it in some form of a knot. Normally they covered their hair with a cloth or a veil. To expose their hair publicly was a disgrace.

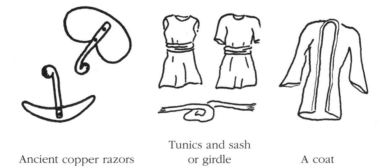

Ancient copper razors   Tunics and sash or girdle   A coat

Clothing of men. Men in Bible times dressed very simply. They wore no underwear or trousers. Their tunic was a long close-fitting woven shirt reaching to the knees. In colder seasons they wore a longer tunic. The tunic had short sleeves or no sleeves at all. The girdle was a sash, made of linen (Jeremiah 13:1), or a belt of leather (John the Baptizer—Matthew 3:4). The outer garment, the coat, appears to have been cut to fit loosely, like a modern dressing gown or bathrobe. A second sash held it in place, either completely closed or partly open in front. Men might use the whole coat to carry grain or other burdens. They would tie it together at the sleeves and corners. They would carry it on the back, as people still do in the East (Exodus 12:34; Judges 8:25). For more formal occasions they wore a coat with long, loosely flowing sleeves. A very broad outer sash of contrasting material held it together at the front. Blue fringes adorned the borders of the garment to remind the Israelites to do all God's commandments (Numbers 15:38–39). Rich men wore finer fabrics, more expensively tailored, and sometimes richly embroidered in colored silk and gold. They maintained a large wardrobe of expensive clothes for their own use or to give to friends or guests.

Originally the cloak probably was a sheepskin or blanket. However, a man's cloak was usually made of woven wool, cotton, or goat's hair. It had dark brown and lighter vertical stripes, sometimes white. Its long flowing lines gave the appearance of increased height. Bedouins still wear this long flowing cloak, which keeps out the cold of night as well as the heat of day. The traveler wrapped his head in the cloak. His legs were bare. At night or in wet weather he could pull his legs up under the cloak. A cloak was very important for the poor. If taken as security for a debt, it could not be kept overnight: "If you ever take your neighbor's garment as a pledge, you shall return it to him before the sun goes down. For that is his only covering, it is his garment for his skin. What will he sleep in? And it will be that when he cries to Me, I will hear, for I am gracious" (Exodus 22:26–27).

Both men and women wore sandals with soles fastened to the foot with leather thongs. The soles were made of leather and sometimes of wood. Likely some wore sandals that completely covered their feet. At times sandals left the toes uncovered. In times of sorrow even King David went barefoot (2 Samuel 15:30); necessity often forced the poor to do so.

Leather sandals   Fiber sandals

The type of headdress worn depended on the time and place in which it was worn. People formed a turban by winding a long towel-like strip of woolen material about the head. Turbans are common in the Near East today, but may not have been in Bible times. To make another headdress people folded a square of cloth into a triangle. They held it over the head with a band of woven goat hair. One triangle fell down the back, and one at either side of the face. A visorlike projection protected the eyes from the glare of the sun.

Turban, and linen headdress held by a woven band of goat's hair

Clothing of women. Women's and men's clothing were very similar. The material of women's clothing had a finer weave, and the dresses were worn longer, reaching the ankles. The girdle was much wider, made of finer material, and had more folds than those worn by men. Wealthier women wore a long coat, or outer dress, made of very finely woven wool, fine linen, or silk. Often it was scarlet, embroidered in gold and costly needlework. (See Psalm 45:13–14; 2 Samuel 1:24; and Ezekiel 16:13.)

These women wore sandals similar to those worn by men of high status, but made from fine badger skin (Ezekiel 16:10).

Isaiah warned the worldly overdressed women of his day that the Lord would take away all their luxurious clothing and ornament. He mentions 21 such items, including "the festal apparel, and the mantles, the outer garments, the purses, and the mirrors; the fine linen, the turbans, and the robes" (Isaiah 3:18–23).

For work around the house or in the fields or vineyard the women dressed like the men. They usually also wore a veil as a protection against the heat of the sun.

Seal and staff

Ornament and jewelry. Besides finely embroidered clothing, men of high station commonly wore two additional ornaments, the seal and the staff. The seal, or signet (Genesis 38:18), was worn in a ring on the right hand (Jeremiah 22:24; Esther 3:10). Men used it to sign letters and documents (1 Kings 21:8) and to seal bags of merchandise (Job 14:17). A staff, also a weapon of defense, served as a symbol of dignity. Babylonians, and probably the wealthy Israelites, had finely carved and engraved staffs. They might cap the head of a staff with gold or other precious metals. Some men in neighboring nations, particularly the wilderness and the desert tribesmen, wore earrings, necklaces, and heavy gold chains. Apparently the Israelites did not wear such ornaments.

Ancient jewelry

Mirror, kohl bottle, tweezers, ointment box

155

Women wore a greater quantity and more elaborate ornaments than did the men. Israelite women wore earrings of gold set with precious stones or inlaid with ivory (Ezekiel 16:12), perhaps with long pendants or medallions (Isaiah 3:19). Some women wore nose rings. These were inserted through one nostril or through the septum between the nostrils (Isaiah 3:21; Ezekiel 16:12). Women also wore elaborate necklaces of precious metal or strings of pearls and other jewels (Ezekiel 16:11; Song of Solomon 1:10), bracelets, and anklets of gold and tinkling ornaments about their feet. These were finely engraved or set with precious stones (Isaiah 3:18–19).

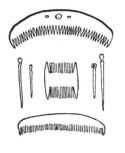

Ancient combs and hairpins

Extremes in the use of cosmetics and adornment. Some women of Israel overdid their ornamentation and makeup. They copied the customs of Egypt and of Babylonia. Some paid exorbitant prices for oils and creams from far countries. They painted their eyebrows and eyelashes. They used so much dark blue eyeshadow, or *kohl,* that they looked extremely artificial. Wealthier women used mirrors of polished bronze (Exodus 38:8). Artificiality affected all aspects of everyday life. The society women of Israel walked "with outstretched necks and wanton eyes, walking and mincing as they go, making a jingling with their feet" (Isaiah 3:16). They deserved the severe censure that Isaiah and Ezekiel gave them. (See Isaiah 3:16–26 and Ezekiel 16:15–23.) Many sophisticated women lived for dress and adornment. They made themselves useless to society and threw themselves open to the temptations that attack those who love themselves above others and even above God.

Ezekiel 16 describes God's goodness to Israel since her birth, including washing, anointing, dressing, ornamentation, etc. Israel misused those gifts for whoredom after false gods and lavish living.

Betrothal and Marriage

The marriageable age. In Bible times no caste restrictions prevented marriage between different classes of Israelites. Nevertheless, people of one social status tended to marry those with similar status. People married when still quite young. Mosaic law does not provide a minimum age for marriage, but by New Testament times Jewish rabbis had set the minimum age for marriage at 12 for girls and 13 for boys. Most considered it a disgrace, or at least a serious disregard of custom and duty, for a man or a woman not to be married by the age of 20. It seems that most young people married about the time they attained their full physical growth—girls by the age of 15 or 16 and perhaps a year older for men.

The contract, or betrothal, as binding as marriage. Arranging a marriage for their children was a basic responsibility of the parents. Thus Abraham arranged for the marriage of his 40-year-old son Isaac (Genesis 24:2–9). Hagar secured a marriage for her son, Ishmael (Genesis 21:21). When Jacob had to flee to Haran, Isaac issued an order about whom he should or should not marry (Genesis 28:1).

Courtship was not part of normal life in the biblical era. It was improper for a boy and girl to be alone together. Community life enabled them to meet others. For example, boys might watch mothers and their daughters going to the village well in the early morning and late afternoon to get water for the family's needs.

When children neared the mid-teens, parents began to plan a proper marriage for them. A young man might give hints to his parents about a desirable candidate(s) for betrothal and marriage negotiations. Finally his parents would decide to explore the possibility of an agreement with the parents of a potential bride. Then a third person would take over the negotiations. Much time could pass before the families agreed what each family would bring to the marriage. Often they put this in writing.

A day of betrothal was set. The negotiator would present a legal contract for both fathers to sign. The young man would then give something of value to his future bride. The marriage itself could not take place sooner than *nine* months after the betrothal agreement had been signed and not later than *twelve* months. During this time the young couple could never be alone together. Should the future bride become pregnant, the future groom could accuse her before the village council (Numbers 5:11–31; Deuteronomy 22:23–24). He could also have a simple divorce document drawn up that he would sign. Two men would take it to her home. This would keep her under the protection of her family. Knowledge of these procedures helps us understand events in the lives of Mary and Joseph (Matthew 1:18–25; Luke 1:26–38).

Sometimes the parents of the future bride or groom wanted to make some changes in the betrothal document. This required renegotiations. After they achieved full agreement, they drew up the marriage document, the *ketubah*.

Marriage involved a lifelong union and obligation for both. Godly people of Bible times carefully followed God's arrangement that "a man shall leave his father and mother and be joined to his wife, and they shall become one flesh" (Genesis 2:24). No one has the right to separate man and wife (Matthew 19:6). The law of Moses recognized divorce, but only people's hardheartedness led to that provision (Matthew 19:8; Mark 10:5–7). Only fornication made divorce allowable (Matthew 5:31–32).

The wedding ceremony; friends of the bridegroom and other attendants. On the day set for the marriage, the bridegroom came to the house of the bride. He was dressed in his wedding garments and escorted by his friends (Matthew 9:15). The girl friends of the bride, as in the parable of the 10 virgins (Matthew 25:1–13), went out to meet them. They also dressed in festive clothing, wearing veils. To prepare for a possible evening event, they carried lamps with which to light the way. The bride greeted the bridegroom at the door. Then she and the whole group went with "the voice of mirth and the voice of gladness" to his home (Jeremiah 7:34).

The signing of the marriage document by both fathers and by the groom was crucial for the ceremony. The bridal couple then drank from a common cup of wine to signify the joy of their life together. Later on this may have taken place under a marriage canopy, the *chuppah*.

The marriage feast. Often many people took part in the marriage feast. They were seated according to their rank or according to the honor the groom wished to show to them (Luke 14:7–9). The group included relatives, neighbors, and visitors who were with the family at the time. The meals were as elaborate as the family could afford. Families considered it a disgrace not to have enough for all. Thus at the marriage of Cana Mary became very concerned when the wine supply ran low. She felt the family suffer disgrace. So she told Jesus, "They have no wine" (John 2:3).

Children

The curse of childlessness and the blessing of children. God's people recognized that "children are a heritage from the Lord" (Psalm 127:3) and that it is the Lord who "grants the barren women a home, like a joyful mother of children" (Psalm 113:9). Hebrew women with no children experienced severe distress (Sarah—Genesis 16:2; Rachel—30:1; and Hannah—1 Samuel 1:6). Such women felt as if they were "a reproach among men," as Elizabeth put it (Luke 1:25). The joy and gratitude of these women, who knew that God answered their prayers by giving them children, show us how bitterly they had suffered (Genesis 21:6; 30:23; 1 Samuel 1:24–28).

While a young mother might welcome the birth of a daughter as a minor blessing, she became radiantly happy when she could present her husband his firstborn son. This boy would continue the family name and would provide strength and support for his parents during their lifetimes

(Psalm 127:3–5). Women of all cultures desire offspring, but a devout Jewish woman of Davidic descent had an added reason. She might be the ancestress of the promised Savior—or perhaps even His mother! People viewed a large family as a very special blessing of God and a sure token of His grace and mercy (Proverbs 17:6; Ecclesiastes 6:3).

Care and nursing of the baby. From early times midwives assisted Hebrew mothers at the birth of their children, as they did for Rachel (Genesis 35:17) and Tamar (Genesis 38:28). In Egypt at the time of the birth of Moses, this profession had been organized into a guild under their own leaders (Exodus 1:15). The midwives noticed that the Hebrew women bore their children with much less pain and delay than did women of Egypt (Exodus 1:19).

Immediately after the birth the midwife bathed the child with warm water and rubbed it with salt and possibly with olive oil. She then wrapped it in swaddling clothes. These were long strips of cloth firmly wrapped about the child's body (Ezekiel 16:2–5; Mary, at the birth of Jesus—Luke 2:7). People believed that a tightly swaddled child would grow stronger and healthier than one left free.

Hebrew mothers took great pride in caring for and nursing their own children (Sarah—Genesis 21:7; Hannah—1 Samuel 1:2–3). Such a precious gift of God could not be left out of their sight. However, in some cases they secured the service of wet nurses (Exodus 2:7).

Ezekiel writes that a wretched infant typifies Jerusalem. "As for your nativity, on the day you were born your navel cord was not cut, nor were you washed in water to cleanse you; you were not rubbed with salt nor swathed in swaddling cloths. No eye pitied you, to do any of these things for you, to have compassion on you; but you were thrown out into the open field, when you yourself were loathed on the day you were born" (Ezekiel 16:4–5).

On the eighth day of his life, even if it fell on the Sabbath, the boy underwent the rite of circumcision, according to God's command. Like our own children who have received Baptism, he now belonged to God's chosen people and was an heir of His gracious promises. At this time the child also received his name. In early times it appears that the name was often related to some personal peculiarity (Esau, the red one—Genesis 25:25) or with a circumstance connected with the child's birth (Benjamin—Genesis 35:18), or with the experiences (Samuel—1 Samuel 1:20) or hopes of the parents for the newborn child (Reuben—Genesis 29:32). At the birth of John the Baptizer the relatives and friends took it for granted that the baby would be named after his father (Luke 1:59–63). No doubt this had become a common practice.

After a period of time (40 days in the case of a boy; 80 days in the case of a girl) the mother went to the temple and offered a sacrifice of purification (Leviticus 12:1–8). Because of her poverty, Mary offered "a sacrifice according to what is said in the law of the Lord, 'A pair of turtledoves or two young pigeons' " (Luke 2:22–24; compare Leviticus 12:8).

Often the mother nursed her child for two or three years. Thus Hannah did not wean little Samuel until she could entrust him to the aged Eli, whom he was to serve at the tabernacle at Shiloh (1 Samuel 1:23). At the time of weaning another family gathering took place, similar to that provided by Abraham when Isaac was weaned (Genesis 21:8).

Early training of children. Children, as special gifts of God and the most precious possession of their parents, enjoyed a happy home life. During the early years the mother took care of the household and provided home training of the children (Proverbs 31). Pious mothers—like the mother of King Solomon (Proverbs 31:1) and the mother and the grandmother of Timothy (2 Timothy 3:15)—brought their little children to the Lord by teaching them His Word. At a very tender age the children heard of the great things God had done for His people. Pious fathers, like Abraham, taught their whole households, including the small children, to "keep the way of the Lord, to do righteousness and justice" (Genesis 18:19).

Moses impressed on God's covenant people the crucial

importance of training children. Children must remember the significance of being members of God's covenant people (Deuteronomy 6:3–9).

Children learned to look forward to the fulfillment of God's promises about the coming Redeemer. They were taught to love, respect, and obey their parents. Most children retain the attitude that develops towards God and their parents during their early childhood years. Few develop wholesome attitudes later in life.

As sons became older, they began to work more with their fathers. Mothers taught daughters to become good future wives and mothers. By helping her mother, a little girl learned to cook. In her own home she observed and took part in all the other household tasks. She learned to sew, knit, spin, weave, grind grain, prepare bread and other foods, sweep and clean the house, and take care of the younger children. By the time she reached even the comparatively early marriageable age, she was equipped to handle a household of her own.

Special training of boys. The term *teacher* has a somewhat broader meaning than we give it today. A teacher might teach in a school or tutor boys privately. He might be a master craftsman in a common trade. A father would ask him to train his sons in that particular trade. A teacher might be anyone highly proficient in his field, whether or not he "taught." Such "a disciple is not above his teacher, but everyone who is perfectly trained will be like his teacher" (Luke 6:40). Only when he has reached this stage of perfection would he dare to be called "teacher" by others. Note what Jesus told His disciples, "One is your Teacher, the Christ" (Matthew 23:10).

In later times, and especially under the influence of Hellenic customs, the boys of wealthy families were turned over to special teachers. Among the earlier Israelites, and perhaps among the poorer classes at all times, the father took care of this duty himself. He taught his sons to read and write well enough to read the Scriptures and to take their rightful place in the community. He carefully continued the religious instruction that he and his wife had begun in the boy's infancy. He also taught his sons how to make their living by a trade, even though the father might earn his living by a profession. Thus Saul of Tarsus, from a good family and trained in all the higher learning of the Jews and Greeks, was by trade a tentmaker. He was not ashamed to support himself at various times during his ministry by working with his hands, along with his converts Aquila and Priscilla (Acts 18:3).

Instead of at school, boys learned trades in the shop at home or in the home of a friend or relative. The sons of farmers learned agriculture by working on the home farm. At a very early age shepherd boys became reliable and efficient enough to be left in complete charge of their father's flocks. Thus the Hebrew boy developed the dignity and privilege of work as well as the need to work to earn a living. He became independent and self-reliant.

Many towns and larger villages had a synagog school for boys. Here they learned to read and write Hebrew. Rabbis emphasized the Old Testament, with special stress on the Pentateuch (Torah) and its instructions for daily life. Schooling began when boys were five or six and apparently continued into the early teens. Especially in the Diaspora they also learned to read Greek. Thus, they could read the Septuagint, the Greek translation of the Old Testament. Their training also involved extensive memorization of key Old Testament passages.

The complete education. Ideally God's covenant people learned that the fear of the Lord was the beginning of wisdom (Psalm 111:10; Proverbs 1:7). This "fear" is a high respect for and love of Him as their God of ongoing grace and mercy. Through the Spirit's work the people avoided evil (Job 28:28) and led a decent and upright life as a dedicated covenant person.

Hospitality, Recreation, and Periodic Festivals

Hospitality and greetings. Bible people, and those in Bible lands today, practiced hospitality. Only a very boorish person would neglect to ask a traveler to stop for a meal or overnight. One should not need to "lodge in the street" (Job 31:32). This traveler might be a stranger. Yet the host invited him in, washed his feet, prepared a meal for him, took care of his donkey or other animal, and treated him like an honored member of the family until he could again send him on his journey. Abraham (Genesis 18:1–8) and Lot (Genesis 19:1–3) showed this hospitality when they "entertained angels unawares." Even crafty and dishonest Laban showed hospitality to his guest, Abraham's old servant (Genesis 24:31–33). When once two Orientals have eaten together, they have formed a bond of friendship that dare not be broken. They are no longer strangers to each other, but there is "bread and salt between them."

When a Hebrew man approached another on the road, he bowed to the ground as a mark of his respect. He dismounted before saluting a stranger while riding on his donkey. Some people of the Near East still do so, after which they fall with the face flat to the ground. People called down the blessings of God on each other when they met in the street. Scripture records a number of such formal greetings: "God be gracious to you" (Genesis 43:29); "Peace be with you" (Judges 19:20); "The Lord be with you" and "The Lord bless you" (Ruth 2:4); and "Peace, peace to you" (1 Chronicles 12:18). After the exchange of the blessing, the host asked about the visitor's health, friends, and family. Occasionally, particularly if those who met were close relatives or friends, the salutation was much more intimate. Scripture records events where men kissed and embraced each other. For instance, Esau "fell on his [Jacob's] neck and kissed him" (Genesis 33:4), a custom that still exists in the Near East. Men embrace with cheeks touching on one side, and then the other. To show respect to older men, young men stood up in their presence (Leviticus 19:32). At the time of farewell the blessing, kissing, and embracing were repeated. Sometimes people also cried (Paul's departure from Miletus—Acts 20:37).

At times people overdo even friendly greetings and hospitality, and the Oriental custom tends to become long, drawn-out, and repetitious. Probably Jesus referred to this when He said to His disciples. "Greet no one along the road" (Luke 10:4). Instead of wasting time in ordinary social obligations and pleasantries, Jesus wanted to proclaim the Gospel. Jesus also said, "Beware of the scribes, who desire to go around in long robes, love greetings in the marketplaces" (Mark 12:38). Note Jesus' own farewell to His disciples. "My peace I give to you; not as the world gives do I give to you" (John 14:27). Deep sincerity dominated over outward formality.

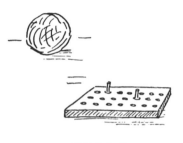

Child's ball and game board

Games and toys of children. As mentioned above, Hebrew parents taught their children the covenant guidelines, respect for their parents and elders, how to do the work about the home and shop, and how to take their places in a world of work and responsibility. However, serious activities did not consume all of a child's time. They played like children play now. They had all kinds of games and toys. Game boards were similar to those used for checkers and various marble games. Children played ball, though we do not know what rules they followed. When a wedding procession with its joyful music and happy party passed by, the children played at "wedding." When a funeral procession wound its way to the grave, the games of the children in the marketplace echoed its solemnity (Matthew 11:17; Luke 7:32). Like girls today, girls played house. Boys played at the trades of their fathers or of others whose activities they had observed. Thus boys and girls sang and chanted and piped and danced with the boundless energy of children everywhere.

Outdoor mass demonstrations, games, festivities of the harvest. On special occasions groups of people gathered at the marketplaces or about the gates of the city for conversation or for recreation (Acts 17:17; Matthew 20:3). At the announcement of a victory or the return of a victorious army, the women went out to meet their returning husbands and sons. They sang and danced, accompanied by cymbals and tambourines (1 Samuel 18:6–7). When Solomon became king, "the people played the flutes and rejoiced with great joy, so that the earth seemed to split with their sound" (1 Kings 1:40). When Jehu became king "each man hastened to take his garment and put it under him on the top of the steps; and they blew trumpets, saying, 'Jehu is king!' " (2 Kings 9:13).

This activity also provided a safety valve for people's pent-up emotions. Such enthusiasm was sometimes short-lived, as when Jesus Himself entered Jerusalem. "A very great multitude spread their garments on the road; others cut down branches from the trees and spread them on the road. Then the multitudes who went before and those who followed cried out, saying, 'Hosanna to the Son of David' " (Matthew 21:8–9).

Various harvest festivals provided opportunity and motivation for rejoicing and group entertainment. The barley harvest came first, followed by the harvest of wheat, grapes, and olives. People worked hard during the day, but music, singing, and sociability brightened their evenings.

Formal entertainment, banquets. A week before a special banquet in celebration of a marriage, a weaning, or the visit of some influential person, the host sent out elaborate invitations. He wanted nothing to prevent the guests from attending. When the day came, the servant of the master repeated the invitation, "Come, for all things are now ready." It was rude to refuse an invitation at any time, but inexcusable to do it at the last moment (the great supper—Luke 14:15–24). When the guests arrived, the host usually greeted them, and his servants washed their feet. Often their heads were anointed, and the host personally conducted them to the banquet hall.

On such a great occasion one might serve "the fatted calf" (Luke 15:23) or a barbecued goat. Hosts spared no money or pains to make it enjoyable for all who attended. Places were carefully reserved for the honored guests, and "social climbers" enviously longed for a better seat (Luke 14:7). Those at the feast engaged in light conversation. Riddles, stories, humor, and music enlivened the festival (Luke 15:23–25; Judges 14:12–18).

Jesus' lessons from the banquet feasts. Since people knew the customs at banquets of the day, Jesus based a number of His teachings on them. He taught a powerful lesson on humility when He noted that the chief places were chosen by the Pharisees (Luke 14:7–14). In the story of the banquet given for the lost son He taught about the joy in the heavenly Father's heart at the return of the sinner and warned against the selfishness of the older brother (Luke 15:11–32). He pictured the joys of heaven as a wedding festival (Matthew 25:1–13). He warned against using the duties and pleasures of everyday life as excuses for putting off our coming to the Lord's great banquet feast (Luke 14:15–24). He taught equality of all by eating with "tax collectors and sinners" like Zacchaeus (Luke 19:1–10) and the mixed company at the feast of Matthew (Mark 2:14–17), as well as with Pharisees and the wealthy (Luke 7:36–50). He called attention to the ruthless rejection of God's grace by the Jews in His parable of the marriage of the king's son (Matthew 22:1–14).

Sickness, Death, and Burial; the Hope of Resurrection

Causes of sickness. Just as sin is common to the whole human family, so are its results, sickness, and death. In general, the climate of Palestine is more favorable than that of other nations of the Near East. Except in the Jordan Valley (which lies from around 700 to almost 1300 feet below sea level and has tropical heat and humidity), Palestine enjoys healthful and invigorating weather conditions. Bible people in general were strong and healthy.

Moses threatened pestilence, consumption, fever, and inflammation, along with other evils, as ways God would lead His people to repentance (Deuteronomy 28:21–22). Sometimes God punished the whole nation (2 Samuel 24:15) or guilty individuals (Gehazi—2 Kings 5:27; Jehoahaz—2 Chronicles 21:18–19) for gross and unrepented sin. See "Medicine and Healing" in chapter 7 for information about some common diseases. A good Bible dictionary will provide more information.

Sympathy in sickness and mourning in death. Sickness of anyone in the family disturbed the whole family. Since people knew so little about disease and its treatment, they approached illness with general fear and even terror. They called a physician if one was available. Often, however, an older member of the community prescribed remedies. God's people also prayed in times of sickness. They knew that God could cure it if it was His will (Psalm 103:3; Matthew 9:21). The whole family crowded into the room in order to show their sympathy. At the bedside of the sick they wept, mourned, and comforted the afflicted one. At the same time they unwittingly robbed the person of peace and quiet, shut out fresh air, and made recovery more difficult.

When a person died, mourning began immediately. Neighbors joined the wailing, and it finally penetrated the whole community. Friends and neighbors visited the bereaved family. They combined weeping and comfort in an uncontrolled flow of emotion. Such demonstrations may seem out of place, but they were sincere. Our Lord Himself was overcome with grief at the tomb of His friend Lazarus, and He wept (John 11:35). This action shows His heartfelt sympathy for all mourners, then and now. "Blessed are those who mourn, for they shall be comforted," He said (Matthew 5:4). The body was immediately prepared for burial, which ordinarily took place on the day of death.

Burial customs. The Israelites knew how Egyptians very carefully and thoroughly embalmed their dead, but they did not usually embalm bodies. They washed the dead, then dressed them or wrapped them in "grave clothes" (Lazarus—John 11:44). They might then sprinkle the clothing or wrappings with sweet-smelling crystals of balm. The body was then laid on a stretcher. Friends or relatives carried it to the burial place (Luke 7:12–15). Those chosen to carry out this last act of kindness considered it a special privilege. The mourners walked along beside the stretcher, weeping and wailing as they went. At the grave they reverently laid the body to rest. Beyond these facts we know very little about the details of the burial.

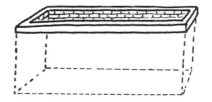

Rock-hewn grave

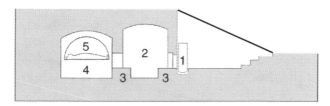

1. The rolling stone
2. The entrance room
3. A narrow shelf was left to serve as a bench
4. The room with graves
5. A grave cut like a bed into the side of the room

Various types of graves were used in Palestine. Abraham bought the cave of Machpelah as a burial place for his wife and family (Genesis 23:15–20). Israelites continued to use caves as burial places throughout their history. When Jesus compared the Pharisees to "whitewashed tombs" (Matthew 23:27), He was referring to the clean, whitewashed slab of limestone that covered the rock-hewn grave containing dead men's bones. Other holes were dug into the side of a rock hill, thus forming an artificial cave. A stone could be rolled in front to serve as a door. Such a stone rolled across and sealed the entrance to the family tomb of Joseph of Arimathea, in which he and Nicodemus buried Jesus (Matthew 27:66; John

19:41–42). It was very heavy. The women who had come to finish the burial rites on Easter morning wondered who would roll it away for them (Mark 16:3). Some of the natural or artificial caves were very large. Bodies could be laid on their shelves or niches. These could be individually sealed in by flat slabs of stone placed in front of them and plastered in around the edges (Mark 15:46).

The hope of resurrection. For believers of Bible times, as well as for Christians today, the grave does not end all. God's people do not sorrow "as others who have no hope" (1 Thessalonians 4:13). We know that God, who created and redeemed us, can and will also raise us from the dead. This truth gave hope to the people in the Old Testament. Job voices this hope in the words, "I know that my Redeemer lives, and He shall stand at last on the earth; and after my skin is destroyed, this I know, that in my flesh I shall see God, whom I shall see for myself, and my eyes shall behold, and not another" (Job 19:25–27). Martha knew that Lazarus will rise again in the resurrection at the Last Day, though she did not realize that her brother would become alive again so soon (John 11:24).

At times God gave prophets the power to raise the dead. Jesus Himself raised the young man of Nain and Lazarus. He promised that He Himself would rise again, and He brought that promise to a glorious fulfillment on Easter morning. Thus, in the Old and the New Testament alike, death has lost its sting, and the grave has lost its victory. The glorious resurrection day points the way to the everlasting home of the people of God.

Review Questions and Exercises

1. What facilities for bathing did people have during Bible times? What kind of material was commonly used for "anointing"?
2. Describe the normal clothing of biblical men. How did this differ from that worn by women?
3. What was considered a proper age for marriage in Bible times? How were marriages arranged?

4. What was "betrothal"? How did this affect marriage?
5. What was the significance of circumcision? Why?
6. What was the role of the home in the education of children?
7. What was the role of the synagog school?
8. What role did hospitality play in the life of people in Bible times?
9. Comment on burial practices and the time of burial in Bible times.

Additional Activities

1. Compare the extremes in women's clothing in the late Old Testament times with those in our civilization today. What principles should guide a Christian women in her choice of clothing, jewelry, and cosmetics? How can the awareness of these principles best be fostered among teenage girls today? Apply similar questions to boys.
2. How do Matthew 1:18–25 and Luke 1:26–38 help you understand New Testament marriage practices? Why are these texts so important for the Christian faith?
3. How do the parables of the 10 virgins (Matthew 25:1–13) and of the wedding feast (Matthew 22:1–14) as well as Genesis 34:11–12 help you understand marriage practices during Bible times?
4. What information do Matthew 27:59–60, Mark 15:46–16:8, Luke 23:53–54, and John 19:39–20:10 provide on New Testament burial customs and tombs?

CONDITIONS FOR CREDIT

1. No fewer than six 60-minute class sessions shall be held.
2. Attendance at 75% of the class sessions shall be required.
3. At least one hour of preparation shall be requested of all students in advance of each of the class sessions.
4. The textbooks and instructors' guides recommended by the Department of Child Ministry of the Lutheran Church—Missouri Synod shall be used.
5. An instructor other than the pastor ought to be approved by the local pastor in order to obtain credit for students. This approval shall be indicated by the pastor's signature on the application blank for credit.
6. The application for credit should be sent to the Department of Child Ministry immediately after the completion of the course.

APPLICATION FOR CREDIT

To be sent to Department of Child Ministry
1333 S. Kirkwood Rd., St. Louis, MO 63122-7295

Name of congregation: _____

Address of congregation: _____
(Street and number or R.F.D.)

_____
(City)   (State)   (Zip)

Name of course for which credit is desired: _____

Dates on which lessons were conducted: _____

_____

Length of class sessions in minutes: _____ Number registered in class _____

The persons on the following list have met all the requirements in regard to attendance, preparation for class work, and final test and are recommended to receive credit.

(Signed) _____ Instructor

Date: _____ (Signed) _____ Pastor

If the instructor of the course is not the pastor of the congregation, there should be two signatures: the instructor's and the pastor's.

(Please type or print)   **Last Name**   **First Name**   **Middle**

1. _____

2. _____

3. _____

4. _____

5. _____

6. _____

7. _____

8. _____

9. _____